space and light

space
and light

how to maximize the potential of your home

katherine sorrell

MITCHELL BEAZLEY

Space and Light
by Katherine Sorrell

First published in Great Britain in 2005 by
Mitchell Beazley, an imprint of Octopus Publishing
Group Ltd, 2–4 Heron Quays, London E14 4JP

ISBN 1 84533 016 1

A CIP record for this book is available
from the British Library

Set in AG Book and AG Old Face
Colour reproduction by Bright Arts HK
Printed and bound in China by Toppan

Senior Executive Editor ANNA SANDERSON

Executive Art Editor AUBERON HEDGECOE

Senior Editor EMILY ANDERSON

Design JOHN ROUND DESIGN

Editor COLETTE CAMPBELL

Picture Researchers CLAIRE GOULDSTONE,
GIULIA HETHERINGTON

Production GARY HAYES

Contents

Introduction

Estate agents may tell us that the most important aspect of a property is its location, but there are other factors that are just as vital when it comes to feeling truly at home. Comfort, charm, integrity, sophistication, an atmosphere of general well-being – these are all pretty intangible, and difficult to define in terms of the usual building and decorating principles, but they are fundamental to what we require from the places we inhabit.

These factors may relate to elements such as the proportions of the architecture, the colours of the rooms, and the style of the furnishings; however, more crucially, they relate to the amount of space in which we live, and how well lit it is. Without adequate space we feel hemmed-in, cluttered, and claustrophobic; with enough space we can spread out, enjoy our possessions (whether stored or displayed), and relax with a sense of luxurious ease – either alone or with company. Light is equally significant: lack of sunlight can make us depressed, while artificial light is not only necessary for safety but also for sending out signals of security, welcome, vitality, and warmth.

Unfortunately, however much you need more space, or a home with better natural light, it's not always possible simply to move to a larger, lighter place. Nor is it necessarily feasible to build an extension, or to convert a loft or basement. Such things take time, planning, and, usually, a fair amount of money. If you're tight on cash, or a tenant rather than a home-owner, and have outgrown your space but are unable to make dramatic changes, you'll need to be more inventive. It doesn't matter whether your home is a city apartment or a country cottage, a new house on an estate or a period property in the suburbs, whether it is tiny or fairly large – you'll still want to maximize its potential. Perhaps your entire space needs re-inventing, or maybe it's just one room that is causing a problem – a narrow hallway, a cramped living room, or a too-small bathroom, for example. But there are always solutions to suit you and your budget.

The starting point is to assess your home thoroughly from top to bottom. Identify the areas that work well, and those that need changing. Don't just look at rooms individually but also how they fit together – do they connect logically and work as a whole? Visual coherence and a functional connectivity is necessary for the spaces to look good and operate on a practical level.

Making the most of space and light is as much about quality as it is quantity. A small home that is nicely proportioned, tactile, well laid-out, and full of character can be a great deal more pleasant to live in than a larger home that is poorly designed, dark, and impersonal. Think carefully about the way you live and your individual needs – don't be bound by how the space has been laid-out in the past. Design your home to suit you personally, both for the way you live now and (if you think you'll be there for a while) in the future. Decide whether you would like, and can afford, professional help from an architect or interior designer: they may pay for themselves in terms of the unexpected solutions they come up with. The next step is to consider the range of space-enhancing options open to you. Some are more drastic than others, but you may feel they are worth the effort. Can you, for example, remove an interior wall and turn two tiny rooms into one large, open one, perhaps with windows at both ends to double the natural light? Can you change rooms around, so that a kitchen benefits from a window with a view while a bathroom makes do with only artificial light? Can you turn a window on an exterior wall into a full-length door – or even create a wall of folding glass doors that lead straight out into the garden?

These ideas may utterly transform your home but would not necessarily come cheap. However, this book concentrates on ingenious, accessible, easy-to-achieve solutions that are, on the whole, near the other end of the scale in terms of effort and financial input. The first section, Elements, examines the different ingredients that you can utilize, either individually or together, to make the most of your space and light. It looks at how colours, patterns, and textures can make a home feel more open and airy; at how using transparent and reflective surfaces creates the illusion of space and bounces light into dark corners; at the styles of furniture that are most space-enhancing; at ways in which to improve your windows and window treatments; at the importance of good storage; and at how to enhance natural light and to install a really effective lighting scheme. The second section, Ideas for living, takes these elements and puts them into context in all the rooms of the house, while the third section, Real homes, gives examples of people who have pushed the potential of their properties to the full, using every available trick to fill them with light and give an impression of the largest possible space. I hope that some or all of these ideas will inspire you and help you to re-think your home to make it function brilliantly, look gorgeous, and feel both comfortable and individual – whatever its style or size.

Elements

Colour, texture, and pattern

The colours, textures, and patterns we use in our homes add dynamism, personality, and richness. They create a particular mood, perhaps calm and serene, cosy and inviting, or fashionable and fun; and they bring a vitality that is both gratifying and uplifting. More than that, though, they can also alter the dynamics of a room, disguising or accentuating features and manipulating the sense of space in a surprisingly powerful way.

Using colour

Whether on the walls, floors, or ceilings, or in the form of fabric or furnishings, colour affects our perception of space dramatically and dynamically. The science of colour is a complex area but on a fundamental level, colours are simply representatives of a particular wavelength on the spectrum of visible light. When all the wavelengths of visible light hit your eye at once you perceive white, and when no wavelengths hit your eye at all you perceive black. This is why, though it may seem like stating the obvious, white rooms are lighter and brighter than black ones.

There is a basic principle of using colour in order to modify the apparent size of a room: pale colours, because they contain lots of white, seem to recede, enhancing a feeling of spaciousness,

while darker colours absorb light and therefore appear more enclosing. Similarly, "cool" colours such as blue and green (or other colours with blue or green in them) are more distancing than "warm" colours such as red and yellow (or colours with a red/yellow tinge). But colour is an incredibly sophisticated tool, and within these simple guidelines there are innumerable options and variations. This means that deciding on a colour scheme can be a complex and confusing task.

The psychology and symbolism of colour Colour is a hugely powerful decorating tool, offering unparalleled visual stimulation and the ability to transform a space instantly – not just in looks but also in atmosphere. Because our responses to colour are so strong, a room can feel cosy and

Left
Vivid colour can add drama and vitality to a small room. Good lighting is essential to avoid a feeling of claustrophobia and, as here, an extensive use of glass, mirrors, and slim or wall-hung furnishings helps increase the sense of space, too.

Right
In this living room pattern is limited to coloured stripes, which complement the strong horizontal lines of the furnishings. With a background of white walls and upholstery, the result is cohesive and sophisticated.

Above
Mauve and orange are
opposites on the colour
wheel, so although this
colour combination is
unexpected, it works well.
Bold shades are best
offset by white or pale
colours, as here.

choices, can live with them comfortably, and feel
satisfied that they make the most of your space.

How to choose colours In general, colour
schemes need to be chosen with various other
references in mind. The age and style of your
home is a good starting point, as some colour
palettes are more appropriate for certain eras
than others (an all-white scheme, for example,
would probably suit a modern apartment but
might be too stark for a Georgian property, which
would benefit from softer shades). The amount of
natural light will be relevant, too, as you can get
away with darker colours in rooms with large
expanses of glass. You will also need to consider
the colours of your existing furnishings which,
unless you are going to re-paint or re-cover them,
will have to be incorporated into the scheme –
perhaps as a focal point, or maybe something
to be disguised or minimized. And, of course,
no choice of colours is ever a totally clear-cut,
logical decision; we are all drawn inevitably
towards particular shades, and feel instinctively
that certain colours will suit us and the space
we inhabit more than others.

   Because covering the walls, ceiling, and
sometimes the floor with a fresh coat of paint
is the easiest, quickest, and cheapest way to
transform a room, this is most people's first
choice. To pick the perfect paint colour, buy a
selection of matchpots and paint each onto large
sheets of thin card. Tape them to the walls all
around the room and live with them for a few
days, observing how the changing light affects
the colours. As well as the shade, carefully
consider the finish, too, as matt emulsion has a
completely different effect to high-gloss (see the
Texture section on pp16–17 for more information).
When choosing fabrics for curtains or upholstery,
obtain as large a swatch as possible and drape
it in place to get the full effect.

Combining colours While it is advisable to keep
the number of colours in a scheme to a minimum,
so as to avoid an unpleasant and space-limiting
visual confusion, a subtle and harmonious blend
of colours will give your scheme a well thought-
out and sophisticated edge. If you don't feel
confident about combining colours, follow some
simple rules – darker and lighter shades of the

inviting or cold and impersonal solely as a result
of the colours used; our reaction is subconscious
but nevertheless compelling. This primitive
reaction to colour stems from millions of years
of evolution, in which colour served as a vital
indication of danger or safety (poisonous
yellow berries or lush green fields, for example).
Colour has the ability to uplift or depress, and can
even produce a physical reaction: the brightest
red induces a faster heartbeat and rate of
breathing, and is an appetite stimulant, while soft
blue causes the body to produce calming
chemicals. Thus, it follows that red may be a good
choice for a dining area, and blue for a bedroom.

   On a cultural level, colour has gained
symbolic meanings that vary around the world,
so that white, for instance, is a traditional colour
for weddings in the West, while it is worn as
mourning in Asia and used to ward off evil in
Africa. However, your own reaction to colour
is entirely personal, and there is no need to be
controlled by traditional associations – it is more
important that you are happy with your personal

same colour always work well, as do colours that are adjacent to or opposite each other on the colour wheel (picture a rainbow curved so that the ends join, making a circle). These could include combinations you might never have otherwise thought of, such as turquoise with midnight blue, fuchsia with crimson, lime green with pink, or blue with orange. Failing that, look at naturally occurring colour combinations, such as in a flower border or rock formation, or – most straightforwardly – there is no shame in copying a scheme that appeals to you from a book or magazine.

Whites and off-whites White was considered an uninspiring utility colour until the late 1920s, when society interior decorator Syrie Maugham created the "all-white room", with white walls, white furniture, and a white floor, and made it all the rage. It subsequently became the defining colour of Modern Movement architecture, thanks to its purity, anonymity, and visual clarity. Because white contains the most light, it is the most space-making of all colours, and rooms that are decorated entirely in white should, in theory, always appear bigger than they really are. However,

in practice it simply would not be possible to live in a room that was pure white from top to bottom: the effect would be like living inside a refrigerator – impossibly cold, stark, and sterile.

White, in any case, is not just one single colour. There are many variations of white, from the blue-white of modern, synthetic paints to the chalky whites of traditional paints, and their subtle differences can be as interesting as the more obviously contrasting shades of bolder colours. And then there are the off-whites – too dark to be considered white, but too pale really to be called a more definite colour – which include ivory, cream, bone, stone, and the once-ubiquitous magnolia. This family of colours (or one might call them non-colours) is simple and minimal. They are timeless and could easily be used in any style of room, and, as well as having the effect of increasing space and light, they make you feel completely calm and peaceful.

Painting the walls, wooden furniture, and flooring all in whites or off-whites, and adding white upholstery and window treatments, would create the basis for a cool and contemporary interior with the optimum sense of space: because the joins between walls, floor, and ceiling

Right
Even a room painted entirely in white contains subtle variations in colour – as the light hits each surface it alters the shade slightly each time. The natural texture of wood is an ideal foil to plain white paint.

Above
A dazzling colour painted
on just one wall can
provide a focal point,
inject drama and
personality, or distract
the eye from a flaw
elsewhere in the room.

would all but disappear and the space would seem almost limitless. This type of scheme could be combined beautifully with natural colours and textures, such as those of timber and stone, to soften the somewhat challenging effect of all-encompassing white. Alternatively, white is the great unifier of other colours – use it on walls to link disparate furnishings, or to tone down a busy room, and as a backdrop to highlights of bold and bright colour.

Living with white Sometimes, of course, real life gets in the way of the ideal notion of painting a small room white all over and installing pristine white furnishings, as anyone with a small child or a dog will know. However, with some ingenuity you may be able to solve the problem. Machine-washable loose covers, pre-sprayed with fabric protector, tough, wipe-clean paint and wallpaper, and carpet with built-in stain guard will all go a long way towards keeping a white room as clean as possible, though the brave person who fits white carpet will undoubtedly want to go one step further and ask anyone entering the house to take their shoes off at the door.

Pales and pastels Less clinical than white, soft, pastel colours are easy to live with and produce a relaxed atmosphere that is calm and welcoming. Because they contain so much white they are almost as effective in increasing a sense of airiness and space, and can be used in all styles of interior, whether traditional or contemporary. As well as paler versions of the primary colours – powder pink, baby blue, and lemon yellow – soft colours include secondary shades such as peach, mint green, and lilac. Using variations of one pastel colour will result in a harmonious room scheme, but it is also relatively easy to combine two or more shades, as they complement each other so easily with no harsh contrasts.

When to use bright or dark colours Though bolder colours are more tricky to use successfully, this does not mean that they should be avoided altogether, as bright colour can make a strong personal statement and dramatically bring a room to life. As a focal point in an otherwise plain room, a spot of bold colour can make the difference between a scheme that is bland and

boring and one that is inspiring and exciting. You could introduce it in the form of a chair, or set of chairs, a curtain or blind, a few cushions arranged on a sofa, a rug, a bedcover, a vase, a painting, or just one wall painted in a vivid hue. As long as you limit the use of strong colour, allowing plenty of white or pale shades in between so it feels like there is room to breathe, the room will still seem spacious but will also feel rich, vibrant, and alive. Another time when you may want to introduce bright or dark colours is when a small room is just that – a small room – and nothing that you do will really make much of a difference. So why not paint the walls a fabulous, vivid colour and create a space that might not feel big, but at least makes a lasting impact? Avoid a feeling of claustrophobia by lighting it well, and using plenty of mirror, glass, and slender furniture.

Below
Soft shades are easy to work with – they look good with any style of property, can be combined without jarring, and, because they contain so much white, will enhance the amount of space and light in a room.

Above
Bathrooms tend to be
full of hard surfaces
and can therefore look
monotonous, especially
when the colour scheme
is almost entirely white.
Introducing varying
textures, such
as towelling, brick, and
brushed and polished
metal, makes the
room more appealing
and comfortable.

Opposite
Despite its plain design
and neutral colour
scheme, this space is
full of interest thanks
to a selection of natural
textural surfaces.

The importance of texture

If you have ever walked into a beautifully decorated room and noticed a strange absence of warmth, comfort, or welcome, then it is possible that the room was lacking in textural contrasts. For a space to appeal on all levels – not just visual, but also physical, emotional, and spiritual – then it must be satisfying to the touch as well as to the eye. Practically, we need different textures around the home for it to function properly (a dimpled, non-slip bathmat, or a soft pillow), but psychologically we also need to relate to our surroundings in a direct and basic way. So choosing a pleasing mix of surface textures is as important as selecting an attractive mix of colours if you are to create a room that is truly enjoyable to live in.

Introducing appealing textures Texture becomes enormously significant when you are restricting your colours and/or using predominantly white or very pale shades in order to increase the sense of space around your home. It enhances or even takes over from colour in terms of creating a structure and defining different areas, and introduces both visual and tactile interest in a way that is at once understated and sophisticated. Good use of texture can save a room from feeling cold or bland, and it is difficult to get wrong. Unlike the potentially tricky subject that is colour, it is hard to overwhelm or over-complicate a space by making bad decisions about texture.

In general, hard textures provide the backbone of a room and soft ones a gentler counterpoint. All you need to do is to layer one texture with another until you reach a gratifying combination. The textures that make a room seem larger are those that reflect the light – smooth, flat, and shiny. Uneven, matt textures, on the other hand, absorb light: think of the difference between silk and felt, varnished timber and driftwood, and gloss and matt paint. So, a kitchen furnished with gloss-painted laminate units will feel bigger than one equipped with limewashed, reclaimed timber cupboards, a sofa upholstered in smooth cotton will appear less imposing than one upholstered in bouclé wool, and a floor laid with smooth rubber will seem more expansive than one covered with ribbed coir matting.

You can have too much of a good thing, though, and while plenty of smooth, one-dimensional textures are useful for throwing light around a room, it's a good idea to temper them with the addition of a few rough, hairy, knobbly, or riven surfaces to provide character, comfort, and contrast. In a living room with a plain carpet, painted wood furniture, a cast-iron fire surround, and cotton-covered sofas, you could, for example, introduce a cushion or two made from knitted wool, velvet, jumbo corduroy, or suede, or a throw made from fake fur, velvet, chenille, or felt. On a shelf or mantelpiece you could place a piece of driftwood or a matt-glazed pot, a papier mâché bowl or a hammered metal candlestick. Just like colours, certain textures go in and out of fashion with the seasons, and swapping simple accessories around will not only offer textural stimulation but also keep your home up-to-date with the current "look".

Above
The delicate, twining floral patterns of these bolsters and cushions bring life to an otherwise very plain bedroom, but because they are so subdued they maintain the room's calm and restful feel.

The problem of pattern

From the Modern Movement onwards both architecture and interiors have tended towards the simple and minimal, which meant that design schemes involving pattern became correspondingly less popular. However, recent years have seen a resurgence of interest in pattern and an increased desire to break away from the predominance of plain colours alone. But patterned surfaces can be problematic: they can make small rooms seem tiny, and even quite large rooms seem busy and cluttered. There is no doubt that introducing pattern to a scheme designed to enhance space and light can be challenging. However, using pattern well is truly rewarding, and if the idea appeals it is worth the

effort, as there is no doubt that patterns provide great focal points, eye-catching character, and unique richness and vitality. In certain circumstances they may even help to change the apparent dimensions of a room, making it seem taller or wider than it really is.

Pattern basics Because pattern is very individual it is difficult to lay down guidelines for using it – what appeals to some will not appeal to others, and there really is no right or wrong. But there are a few basic principles to consider. It is important to remember that there is pattern in everything, from the geometry of a window surround to the horizontal lines of a low sofa, from the whorls and grain of natural wood to the squares and rectangles of mirror edges and picture frames. So take a long, hard look at your room and consider which patterns are already present before deciding what others to introduce. You may wish to echo the inherent patterns, or to complement or soften them by using a contrasting design.

Different effects can be created by different types of pattern, whether small and delicate or oversized and bold. Stripes are useful for delineating or even altering a space (see p21), and can be monotone or multicoloured, narrow or broad, close together or wide-set. They are versatile and easy to use, as are checks, which vary from tiny gingham to tartan or large-scale windowpane. Other geometric and abstract patterns range from straightforward to complex – simple spots or organic shapes to full-on, intricate designs that really make an impact.

Florals tend to be more popular in older, traditional properties, but can also be an attractive feature in a modern home. As well as bright and blowsy chintzes, you can choose from petite sprigs and stylized, graphic blooms in just one or two colours; they look less girly when combined with stripes and/or checks. Pictorial patterns, such as *Toile de Jouy* or *trompe l'oeil* images, are best used in plain colourways and small doses, perhaps combined with simple geometrics but never with florals (as the two designs would clash with each other). Exotic patterns, such as ethnic designs or animal prints, can look marvellous in a contemporary interior as a focal point in an otherwise neutral scheme. Whatever patterns you choose, bear in mind that a simple colour palette will always give you more flexibility, and will prevent the scheme from becoming overwhelming.

Pattern in small rooms When choosing a pattern for a restricted space, consider its proportion

Below
A pattern of painted squares and rectangles, in strongly contrasting colours, is a simple way to introduce character and vitality to a mainly monochromatic room scheme.

very carefully: in general, use small patterns in small rooms and reserve larger patterns only for larger rooms. A small space is easily overwhelmed by huge, brightly coloured patterns, though it may sometimes be effective to introduce a small section of large-scale pattern – as a print on one wall, for example, or as a striking cushion cover or blind. A tiny pattern, on the other hand, is only really noticeable close up; from a distance it will appear simply as the dominant colour, making this a subtle addition to a scheme that emphasizes a sense of spaciousness but nevertheless calls for a decorative element. It is always worth looking at a pattern from a distance before using it, as

many designs look entirely different at close range than when viewed from afar.

Combining patterns Putting two or more patterns together calls for confidence but can result in a highly sophisticated, coherent scheme – or a dreadful, visually confusing mess. To achieve the former and avoid the latter, limit the number of patterns you use according to the size of the room. In a small room it is wise to opt for only one or two patterns, to avoid them becoming a distraction. Choose patterns with the same colours (a really good match, not just an approximate one) and do not mix very large with very small prints – the eye finds the jump too

Left
The bold stripes of this
rug create a focal point
and define the dining
area. Because so much
white is used elsewhere,
the effect is interesting
rather than overwhelming.

Opposite
If you are using a material
with an inherent pattern,
such as this emphatically
grained wood, it makes
just as strong a statement
as any print, wallpaper,
or paintwork.

disturbing. Instead, use small with medium, or medium with large. Two very dense patterns will probably fight one another, so it's usually best to team one busy pattern with one or two others that are much simpler – a floral with a stripe or check, for example – and tone the whole look down by breaking up and balancing the patterns with large expanses of plain colour as a background.

Space-making tricks with pattern The eye is naturally attracted to patterns as opposed to plains, which is why they are such a potent tool. For this reason, when used cleverly they can help fool the eye into believing that a room is bigger than it really is. With pattern you can draw attention from, say, a low doorway, by putting an intricate wallpaper on the wall opposite, or you could create a focal point with some mosaic tiling

in a bathroom in order to lessen your awareness of its tiny proportions. In a narrow room you can fake a feeling of width by using horizontal lines across the walls, perhaps in the form of wallpaper, fabric, paint, or a row of pictures.

Flooring, too, is particularly effective in this case – either floorboards (which have their own linear emphasis) or carpet or vinyl with a linear pattern can be laid to run across the narrowest width of the room to make it seem wider. Similarly, pattern is effective in making low-ceilinged rooms appear higher: vertical stripes, or patterns that have a vertical feel, will elongate the lines of the room – an optical illusion that can be created equally well by wallpaper, paint, fabric, or tiles. The stripes do not have to be big and bold – they could be faint and subtle and still have the desired effect.

Storage

Storage is important in any home, but in a house that is short of space it is absolutely vital. Without well-planned storage, rooms can seem cramped, messy, and uncomfortable; with it they feel ordered, calm, and spacious. Once everything is in its rightful place – whether behind closed doors or out on display – you reduce stress and clutter, and maximize space for enjoyable and relaxed living.

Organize and assess

Before you start planning what type of storage to put where, you must assess your storage needs. First, go through the house, room by room, and make piles of everything you no longer need or want. You may be able to sell some items, and others can be given to charity; some things can be recycled, and the rest thrown away.

Now consider everything that needs storing, and where it should go. Accessibility is the main factor – things you use daily must be closer to hand than things you only need once a week, while those items you get out just once a year (Christmas decorations, snowboarding gear, and such like) can be tucked into out-of-the-way places such as the back of high shelves or in the loft. In every room you will have the option of different types of storage, and by taking account of what you have and how often you need to get to it you will have a better chance of creating a storage scheme that works perfectly for you.

Have a masterplan A storage plan is highly individual, and how much you need, where, and what it looks like depends very much on how you live. Do you, for instance, like to show off

Right
A series of symmetrical niches is a convenient, tidy way of storing hi-fi equipment and CDs. Painted in vivid colours and with inset lighting, they also make a fun display in their own right.

your possessions on shelves or in glass-fronted cabinets, or do you prefer to hide things in cupboards, chests, and boxes? The latter option will help to streamline the space and give the impression that the room is larger than it really is; however, only the most ardent minimalist would advocate living without at least a few personal possessions on show around them.

Have you got a surfeit of shoes, a lot of bathroom lotions, several spare duvets, or a couple of cat baskets? And what about other requirements, such as housing a prized collection, keeping fragile or perishable items safe, or ensuring that dangerous chemicals are out of children's reach? All such questions must be considered carefully.

When planning your storage you will need to have an overview that takes into account your style of living and the number and type of possessions to be stored. Work out what you want to display, and what you want to hide, how often you need to get to things, and where it's most practical to keep them. If you find that certain things never seem to get put away where they belong, perhaps you are storing them in the wrong place – it may be more logical to keep a laundry basket in the bedroom rather than the bathroom, or to put your

board games in the living room rather than in a child's bedroom.

It's often a good idea to have a consistent storage theme that echoes either the architectural style of your home or the decorative scheme that you have chosen (such as Georgian detailing on cupboard doors, or the use of woven baskets throughout, for example). And whatever you decide on, remember the golden rule of storage: you can never have too much. Always design with the future in mind, so that there is room for expansion when – as is inevitable – you need it.

Built-in storage

There are many advantages of built-in storage, the main one being that you get exactly what you want – whether it's shelving across a wonky alcove or a cupboard in the eaves. Specially built storage can be made to fit wherever you want it to, and is the only way to make full use of awkward, "dead" spaces. What's more, it can be designed to your exact specifications, so the outside will exactly suit the style of your home and the inside will be a perfect fit for whatever you want to put in it. Its disadvantages, on the other hand, are that it tends to be rather expensive, and, of course, impossible to take with you if you move.

Where to install built-in storage Shelves, cupboards, and wardrobes can be built-in almost anywhere, and they are useful for the obvious spaces – such as the two alcoves either side of a chimney breast or in the area under the stairs – but there are also other ingenious places that you may not have otherwise considered useful. On a landing or in a hallway, for example, you could build tall, shallow cupboards with plain fronts (perhaps raised off the ground so you don't appear to lose floor space) and paint them the same colour as the walls.

The same principle could be applied to an entire wall in a small living room or bedroom. Though it may seem to be taking up unnecessary space, adding copious storage will, in fact, allow you to clear the room of anything that's surplus to requirements and so make it actually seem larger. In both cases, avoid visually distracting handles or knobs – instead fit magnetic push-touch catches so that the cupboards become almost invisible.

Look high up to find further space to fit storage. A good place is above (and perhaps also around) doors and windows, over the lavatory or on the wall above a set of stairs – all areas which would otherwise be wasted. In a room with sloping ceilings, you could have triangular shelves or cupboards built to fill the gaps.

Think about other redundant areas, too, such as an unused fireplace, the back of a door, or beneath a basin, for example. Inventive and unexpected storage could be installed in the treads of a staircase or in the cavities of a false wall. For an even more drastic solution you could even lower the ceiling or raise the floor in order to create more storage space, but always weigh up whether the benefits will be worth the time and expense.

One warning: wherever you decide to fit storage, be careful that you don't block off sockets, switches, taps, and other essentials; if necessary, move them first.

Making it to measure Use cupboards, chests, and wardrobes to hold and conceal all your clutter, from clothes to kitchen equipment, shaving foam to sports kit. These containers can be tall and thin, short and wide, square or asymmetrical, arranged against one wall or built

Opposite
Attractive kitchen equipment (preferably colour-co-ordinating) can be displayed on a series of open shelves, with less aesthetic items stored behind closed doors below.

Right
Without plenty of storage children's bedrooms are in danger of becoming a disaster zone. These boxes are brilliant: easy to access, attractive, and, with the painted alphabet, educational, too.

around a corner, and can be enhanced with pretty knobs, handles, and pulls, or made more subtle with invisible push-open mechanisms or simple, small, round finger holes. A good carpenter can build them to your exact measurements, with shelving, rails, or hooks inside at whatever spacing you require, either using inexpensive wood or medium-density fibreboard (MDF) that you can paint to match your walls or co-ordinate with your decorative scheme, or in more expensive wood that will create a focal point in itself. If you want to make a feature of the doors buy reclaimed, carved, or panelled ones, and design the cupboards around them. However, in small spaces you can make more room by fitting folding or sliding doors, ones that work on a central pivot, small double doors, or even a pull-down blind, as opposed to more traditional hinged doors.

Floor-to-ceiling cupboards make the most of every inch of space, though in some circumstances you may be able to suspend a shallow cupboard, using concealed brackets or bolt fixings, so that it seems to hover above the ground. This will maximize the apparent floor area of the room. Remember that containers hung at eye level seem to take up more room than those that are either higher or lower – and the advantage of sturdy, low cupboards is that they can also be used for seating.

Shelving This is perhaps the most versatile form of storage, though the major drawback is that whatever you put on it is on view, so shelves need to be carefully chosen, kept tidy, and dusted regularly. However, open shelves tend to look less oppressive than lots of large, solid-fronted cupboards, as long as you don't pack them with clutter. The best-looking shelving is fitted wall to wall, with concealed supports, though in certain situations (inside cupboards, or in a laundry room or home office, for example) height-adjustable shelving on vertical supports is useful. Shelves can also be fitted across unused corners.

You can build shelves from a range of materials, including solid wood, MDF, metal, and glass. The latter will make the room look most airy and bright, though these shelves must be made from safety glass at least 10mm ($^{1}/_{2}$in) thick, with the edges ground smooth. If you are really tight on space glass shelves can even be fitted across a window without blocking out the light.

When building a shelf, always ensure that the wall will be able to hold the load of both the shelf and whatever you plan to put on it (books, in particular, are enormously heavy) and, to prevent the shelf from sagging, fit supports at frequent intervals. Avoid building deep shelves high up, as you won't be able to reach the back of them. If you have a number of small objects that you wish to display (slender vases, postcards, paperweights, for example) you could fit a very narrow shelf along an entire wall – it will look attractive without reducing your space. A neat, light-enhancing trick is to line the back of shelving with mirror, and you may also wish to fit shelf lighting, which can transform a dark void into a bright display area.

Free-standing storage

Off-the-shelf storage comes in an almost unlimited variety of shapes and sizes, from plastic shopping baskets to old school trunks, multi-drawer apothecaries' chests to woven willow log baskets, so it should not be too difficult to find pieces that both suit your look and function efficiently. Free-standing storage could be antique or modern, large or small, conventional or unusual – whatever works best for you and your house. On the whole it is cheaper than custom-built storage, though you may have to shop around before you find the perfect piece. Another major advantage is that it is portable, whether from room to room if your storage requirements change, or from one home to another if you move.

Hanging storage If you are lacking in floor space then the obvious alternative is to make as much use of the walls and ceiling as possible. Get large, flat items out of the way – everything from bicycles to folding tables and ironing boards – by suspending them from large hooks screwed well into a strong wall. The beauty of this arrangement is that you can place the hooks at whatever

Opposite
This huge wardrobe has plenty of room for clothes and shoes, but with its simple design and plain doors it's not too visually imposing. It also doubles as a room divider.

Above
This simple antique chest is a beautiful piece of furniture in its own right, and makes a stunning counterpoint to the restrained white fitted cupboards adjacent to it.

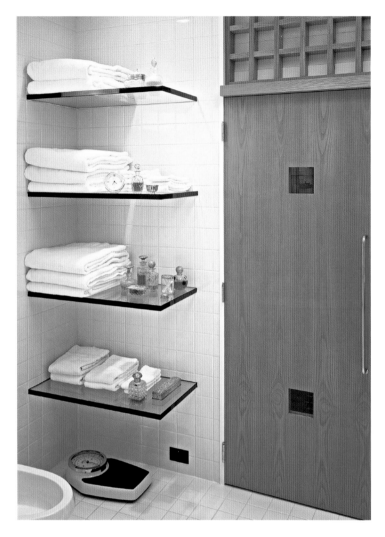

Above
Concealed fittings
make these glass shelves
appear to float, and they
have the capacity to
hold plenty of towels
and toiletries without
appearing to take
up any space.

board in a home office. In the kitchen, a hanging
rail plus "S" hooks or a ceiling rack on pulleys
are useful for pots and pans and a range of
implements, while over-door hooks are perfect
in a bathroom for towels, or in a bedroom for
dressing gowns and smart dresses that won't fit
into a wardrobe. You can also use them to hold
canvas or plastic organizers, which, depending
on their configuration, could hold shoes, folded
shirts or sweaters, toys, tools, or a whole range
of hard-to-store items.

Cupboards, chests, and cabinets Whatever
your storage needs you can be sure that there
will be a free-standing cupboard, cabinet, or
chest of some sort that will answer them. It
could be old or new, large or small, fancy or
plain, made of wood, metal, plastic, or even
heavy-duty cardboard. If you prefer a traditional
look, how about a French armoire, an old kitchen
dresser, or a pine blanket box? For a more
modern effect you might choose a zinc-plated
locker, a white-painted wardrobe, or a chrome
bathroom cabinet. Whether you have scoured
the antique shops, found a retro designer classic,
or gone for department-store simplicity, choose
something that complements the style of your
property and the rest of your furnishings. As for
size, well, it really does matter. Go for the biggest
you can get – as long as it does not overpower
everything else in the room and fits its allotted
space neatly it's no problem if it's half-empty, as
you can be sure it won't stay that way for long.

The great thing about cupboards, cabinets,
and chests of drawers is that they are easy to
customize. If you don't like they way they look,
you can paint them or even cover them with
sticky-back plastic or wallpaper; you can change
the knobs and handles, line glazed doors with
fabric, or remove the doors entirely. Very large
cupboards can be minimized by painting them
the same colour as the walls so they all but
disappear. Of course, I wouldn't advise you to
do any of this to a valuable antique.

Just as you can change the look of a
cupboard, cabinet, or chest, try not to be
constrained by its intended use. If a kitchen
dresser is useful and looks good in a hallway,
that's great. And if a blanket box will hold old
files in your home office, that's fine too. You

heights you like. If the things that you plan to
hang are going to be on view, make sure they are
attractive and well-organized; otherwise hide them
behind a plain canvas cover, curtain, or blind.

An alternative to screw-in hooks are those
with a peel-off sticky back, which are lightweight
but useful for small items – perhaps handbags
arranged on the inside of a wardrobe door, for
example. Suction hooks are useful in a bathroom,
as they can be attached to glass, mirror, and
ceramic tiles without drilling (and the possibilities
of damage that entails), and can be moved
around at will. Use them for flannels, and to hold
little shelves or baskets for shampoo, soap, and
other bathtime essentials. Magnetic hooks can
be attached to a fridge to hold tea towels or a
calendar, perhaps, or maybe on a steel notice-

might find a use for an office cabinet in a bathroom, or a locker in a bedroom – it's up to you, not the manufacturer or retailer.

Though you will find an enormous choice of free-standing container storage, the type you buy will have a marked effect on the feeling of spaciousness in a room. Look for examples that are as tall and slim as possible – they'll have the same capacity as something shorter and wider but will take up less floor space. Choose slender, plain pieces that are subtle in their styling; if they're raised on legs it helps generate a feeling of airiness around them. And storage that works extra hard means you'll need less furniture overall: sturdy, low cabinets and chests, for example, can also double as extra seating if you simply pop a cushion on top, while tall, wide cabinets can become a room divider-cum-storage unit where necessary.

Boxes and baskets As well as making great storage accessories, boxes and baskets can often be attractive elements in a decorative scheme. Boxes may be made from cardboard, acrylic, wood, leather, plastic, nylon mesh, hessian, fabric, or metal, while baskets may be woven in rush, willow, seagrass, rattan, or even telephone wire – there are so many different materials, colours, and textures to choose from that it really isn't hard to find something that both functions effectively and enhances the look of your home.

Left
When choosing furniture for a small room look out for pieces that serve more than one function, such as this coffee table that also has a concealed space for storing newspapers and magazines.

Above
Rows of identical baskets are a smart way of storing folded clothing in a bedroom or dressing room, but can also be used for all kinds of household paraphernalia in the bathroom, kitchen, hallway, or home office.

Boxes and baskets are incredibly useful for storing all sorts of items, from magazines and bedlinen, to toys and out-of-season clothes. They look as good in a living room or bedroom as in a bathroom or home office, and they are great space-savers as they come in so many sizes, from the tiniest jewellery box to the largest laundry hamper, so you can choose exactly what you need. If you can stack them then so much the better for creating extra space, though remember that it will be time-consuming to get items out of the boxes at the bottom.

Other space-making options are large, flat boxes on wheels that roll under the bed, small boxes that can be hung on the wall, boxes that double as seats or foot rests, boxes that nest inside each other when not in use, and baskets that can sit on shelves (the most obvious place is the kitchen, but it could be anywhere) and keep their contents tidy. If you have a lot of things

in boxes, either label them very clearly or buy transparent boxes so you can see what's inside.

Baskets can be bought very cheaply off the shelf, but if you have a specific requirement you could perhaps find a basket-maker who will weave some to your measurements. And don't think you necessarily have to buy special boxes that are designated for storage – some really attractive storage started out life as something entirely different: school trunks, colourful hat boxes, shoe boxes (cover in groovy retro wallpaper to give them more glamour), or even matchboxes, fruit boxes, or egg cartons. In such cases, humble beginnings can lead to beautiful, and useful, endings.

Working wardrobes Space to store clothes can be a problem, but whether your wardrobe is fitted or free-standing there are plenty of clever ways to make it work really hard for you. The conventional wardrobe has a single rail fixed across the top and, if you're lucky, a shelf above. This is fine to store mainly dresses and long skirts but is not so useful for folded items or shirts. If you can find room elsewhere for longer items (perhaps on a large hook screwed to the back of the wardrobe or bedroom door), then another rail, at half-height, would instantly double the wardrobe's capacity.

There is an endless variety of internal fittings that either you can specify, for a made-to-measure wardrobe, or buy off-the-peg for an existing wardrobe. Choose from drawers of different depths, either solid or perhaps made of wire mesh; tie rails, racks, or carousels; canvas hangers with pockets; trouser hangers; shoe racks; jewellery and make-up trays; and stacking boxes in a variety of shapes and sizes, suitable for storing anything from sweaters to rolled-up belts. Ensure that not an inch of space is wasted, remembering to label boxes carefully so that you can find everything easily whenever you need it.

Inspired storage solutions For really unusual and effective storage solutions, look outside the conventions of the domestic arena and take some ideas – and perhaps buy the actual equipment, too – from office, catering, industrial, and retail fixtures and fittings. You may be able to use glass cabinets, metal racks, deep drawers, trolleys, braced shelving, lockers, plan chests, or filing cabinets, and they will have the added advantage of being sturdy, solid, and durable. Of course, much will depend on the style of your home, but industrial items can look fabulous in a modern scheme. However, if you don't want them on show in a living room, you could perhaps find use for them in a kitchen, bathroom, or home office.

Creating an entire wall of shelving in one room may enable you to create more space in other rooms – you could install cupboards, as discussed earlier, or line the wall with shelves, or perhaps put up pegboard (paint this hardboard a bright colour for a quirky, modern look), or an array of hooks. Storage on wheels can also be extremely useful, and it is well worth considering fixing large wheels to the bases of boxes, chests, or other units. And, of course, trolleys are ideal in both bathrooms and kitchens, whether they are made of wood, metal, or plastic. In fact, storage designed for the bathroom is often really ingenious, and there is no reason why you shouldn't use it

elsewhere in the home: corner shelf-towers on adjustable chrome poles could be useful in a pantry, while little plastic shelves on suction pads might be just the thing in a playroom or a work space. Some shower curtains come with pockets for holding soap and shampoo; you could modify this idea for the curtains in a child's bedroom, too.

Finally, study everyday objects with a fresh eye and try to find things that will augment and improve your storage. Instead of seeing bulky luggage as a problem, turn it into a solution by keeping seldom-used items inside it. Look at your cupboards: are you using every inch of space or could you squeeze in an extra shelf or add some useful hooks? Could a door-back canvas shoe organizer be used for office stationery, or clean tin cans or glass jars be transformed into handy containers for toys, tools, or kitchen gadgets? Think carefully, and laterally, and an endless number of storage possibilities will become apparent.

Furniture

Even a large house can feel cramped if it's filled with too much badly chosen and wrongly positioned furniture, while in a tiny property it may seem almost impossible just to fit in all the pieces necessary for daily life. To make any-sized space feel comfortable and look attractive, it's vital to choose items of furniture that work cleverly for your home.

Choosing and using furniture

The first rule of choosing furniture for a small home is to have as little as possible. Pare down to what you really need, questioning the function of each piece. Unless it is essential, get rid of it. To minimize the impact of what's left, ensure that it is simple in style and has a certain consistency, so that shapes, sizes, colours, and textures are linked across the areas – in this way your furniture becomes a seamless whole rather than a disparate, jarring variety of styles.

You should also work out where your furniture ideally should be placed, if necessary drawing scale plans on graph paper, or cutting templates from newspaper and moving them around a drawn plan of the room. Don't be bound by details such as sockets, TV aerial plugs, or telephone points – you can usually have these moved quite cheaply and easily, and it may make an enormous difference to the way you live. If convention doesn't work for you, ignore it: a pair of small sofas facing each other may well be more suited to your lifestyle than a traditional sofa and two armchairs, seating just as many people in less cumbersome a fashion. And don't try too hard to shoehorn off-the-shelf furniture into awkward areas, as it may end up simply looking out of place; a better option might be to have something built to fit – perhaps a desk across a corner, a seat below a bay window, or a wardrobe in an alcove – or to invest in some specially designed furniture that will really suit the space.

Right
A corner sofa may be the best way to utilize your space. This example is streamlined and unfussy, but nevertheless comfortable. The slender metal legs allow you to see underneath, thus increasing the apparent floor area.

Above
Sleek, slender furniture
already has minimal
impact, but when it is
made from a translucent
material, such as glass
or acrylic, it is even
less obtrusive.

Clever designs For real space-enhancing
solutions seek out items that are as unfussy as
possible, and preferably relatively slender and
streamlined in style. It depends on the piece, of
course, as a comfy armchair will need to be soft
and well-padded, or a dining table large enough
for you and some friends to sit at, but in general
avoid over-deep upholstery, bulky outlines, and
ornate detailing. Furniture that is white or pale-
coloured is good, as is see-through furniture
(it could be made of glass, acrylic, or wire, for
example, or perhaps pierced with holes) or
reflective furniture – made from metal, mirror, or
simply given a coat of metallic paint. Anything
raised on legs, whether a sofa, kitchen cupboard,
or bath, will make the room seem larger as it
increases the amount of visible floor area. So,
too, does furniture that is lean and low – with
more room above you the ceiling feels higher,
and low furnishings also minimize what's on
view at eye level. However, conversely there are
times when it is more appropriate to choose
tall, thin furnishings: storage pieces, for example,
will fit into a smaller floor space if that shape,
and yet still hold the same amount of belongings.

Off the wall Just as furniture raised on legs makes a room's floor area appear larger, so does furniture that's hung from the wall. This is effective in a bathroom, where wall-hung basins, lavatories, bidets, and cabinets are readily available in a range of styles. In the kitchen you may be able to hang appliances, such as microwaves, washing machines, or ovens, on strong brackets, while TVs can be mounted on swivelling brackets – as can stereos, DVD players, and speakers. Storage cabinets can also be screwed to the wall anywhere in the house, saving space on the floor for other things.

Dual-purpose furniture Why have two pieces of furniture when one will do just as well, costing less and taking up half the amount of space. The sofa bed is the king of dual-purpose furniture, but there are all sorts of other items that serve more than one purpose, some designed as such but others that easily can be adapted. You might choose a dining table with a cutlery drawer at each end, or a coffee table with integrated space for magazines. A built-in

bench seat could double as a storage chest for toys, a stool could be a side table, or a chest of drawers used as a TV stand. For rooms that need to be divided, a set of open shelves will screen off one area while providing space for books, and two sidetables pushed together could become a convenient dining table. With a little lateral thinking, all sorts of furnishings can lead a double life.

Hideaway pieces In the tightest of spaces it is simply not possible to have all of your furniture out all of the time. A classic example is the dining table and chairs – great if you're entertaining, but redundant (and in the way) the rest of the time. In a studio apartment you may want a sofa out during the day and a bed up at night, while if you work at home you may need to use a computer in the bedroom but want to conceal your office before you go to sleep. Hideaway furniture is the answer – pieces that can be hidden in a convenient space, perhaps flat against the wall, elevated on hooks, hoisted up to the ceiling, tucked under the bed, or secreted in a cupboard.

Below
Dining tables are often a space issue, but this example is minimal in style and, when pushed against the wall, uses very little room; it can also double as a desk when necessary.

Foldaway beds are a good solution to a space problem: they are simply pulled down from the wall when wanted (and they don't even have to be made up each night as a sofa bed would). Foldaway tables and ironing boards can follow the same principle, or you can buy dining tables with drop leaves or gate legs that mean they take up very little floor area. They could be teamed with folding or stacking chairs, or chairs with a hole in the back rest that could be hung from a peg rail on the wall.

If you have a fixed-size table with limited room around it, buy stools instead of chairs and push them underneath when not wanted. For moving all but the lightest furniture on a regular basis, castors are useful (choose the kind that can be locked once the piece is in place). Finally, you may want to consider some of the more ingenious hideaway options, such as a home office that folds out of a large cupboard, or even a kitchen in a box that disappears behind a pair of doors.

Compact choices You can find scaled-down alternatives to all sorts of home furnishings. Kitchen appliances are the obvious starting point, and bathroom manufacturers now offer plenty of options too. In the living room a two-seater sofa may make more sense than a three-seater (three people on a sofa is always uncomfortable, anyway), while a smart suede cube may be a better seating option than a big armchair. It does depend on how you live. For example, if you entertain a lot, a small oven and dishwasher will simply be annoying, and if you have a family you won't manage with a slimline washing machine. If you like to stretch out with your feet up on the sofa, then get as long a one as you can and, whatever you do, never compromise on the size of your bed. One last word of caution: don't furnish your entire house with compact pieces; use them where you really need them, but go too far and your home may end up looking like a grown-up toytown.

Mirror and glass

Glass and mirror are vital in designing a home that maximizes light and space. They dissolve walls and virtually eliminate boundaries, brighten dark corners, and introduce a sense of transparency that dramatically improves even the tiniest of rooms. Accessories and small areas of glass or mirror are effective and attractive, but for a really impressive transformation be bold and use large expanses, wall-to-wall or floor-to-ceiling, as intrinsic architectural elements.

Using mirror

Although we use mirrors every day to check our appearance, they are even more valuable as a way of creating the illusion of larger rooms. This is nothing new – in 17th-century Europe developments in glass- and mirror-making led to a vogue for larger mirrors that were placed precisely in order to enhance the appearance of the room and produce the desired reflection. This culminated in the extraordinary adornment of the Hall of Mirrors in the Palace of Versailles, France.

Today mirrors are no longer an attention-grabbing status symbol; if anything, we want them to disappear quietly into the background and do their job discreetly. However, they are the supreme deceivers of the decorating world, adding depth where it does not exist and doubling the apparent size of a space. They can be used anywhere, from hallways to living rooms, bathrooms to bedrooms, and even in the garden. The key thing is to choose the location with care: a mirror placed opposite a window will distribute the maximum amount of natural light; alternatively, it could be positioned near a light fitting to reflect its brilliance across a room. What you can see in a mirror is also important: choose your view carefully, whether it is of the garden, a painting, a corner of the kitchen, or just a coloured wall.

Sheet mirror The most striking way to use mirror is as large, seamless sheets that cover vast stretches of wall. Fortunately it is easy, and relatively cheap, to have sheet mirror cut to fit your exact needs; then you can either simply glue it to the wall with building adhesive (the most attractive method, as the fixing is invisible) or attach it using mirror clips, or screws with mirror covers. Choose a mirror with safety backing to ensure that it does not shatter into sharp pieces should it be broken. Sheet mirror can be used on one side of a narrow hallway, in an alcove in the bedroom or the sitting room (perhaps behind shelves of books), as a splash-back behind worksurfaces in the kitchen (no crevices for dirt to hide in, and easy to wipe clean), or, perhaps most effectively, in a toilet or bathroom above a washbasin or bath,

Left
Instead of a solid wall, a precisely cut sheet of thick glass has been installed alongside this staircase, opening it onto the hallway while still ensuring safety. Its plain and simple look works perfectly with the unfussy, modern surroundings.

Right
Mirror and glass work in perfect harmony in this clever bathroom, so that it is hard to tell just where the room ends. A glass-sided bath/shower must be very carefully installed in order to avoid leaks.

It can be interesting to play around with the traditional idea of a mirror, so that instead of a single one perhaps hang a pair of identical mirrors, or a group of three or four. For an eclectic look you could even hang a collection of different mirrors on one wall and create a multitude of reflections and an interesting display all in one.

Mirror frames should be chosen with care, so that they don't draw too much attention to themselves but co-ordinate well with other furnishings. Unless you are aiming for an unusual effect, they should also be in proportion with the size of the mirror itself.

Mirror tiles Mirror tiles can be a quick, easy, and inexpensive alternative to sheet mirror in awkwardly shaped areas, or to make a decorative statement with, via the gridded outline of their edges. Use them as you would ceramic tiles, on bathroom walls in particular, though they can also make unusual splashbacks in kitchens and can be used in any other area around the house where there is a flat, dry wall for them to adhere to.

Tiles vary in size, with the smallest being pretty mosaic squares, which come either loose or, more usually, on a mesh cloth or paper sheet. Depending on where you are installing them, it may be possible to avoid grouting between the tiles and simply to butt them up against each other, which results in a more contemporary appearance.

Mirrored furniture Even furniture can be used as a reflective surface, so that solid forms melt away and, instead, reflect the area around them. Mirrored furniture tends to have one of two very specific looks: either Venetian glamour, with etched glass detailing – which is pretty in a feminine though potentially fussy way – or 1930s Art Deco, with bevelled edges and a plainer, more solid look.

In theory, any furniture other than seating can be mirrored, though in practice the most commonly found pieces are for the bedroom, usually in the form of chests of drawers, bedside tables, consoles, and dressing tables. There's no reason, though, why you could not use a mirrored coffee table in the living room, a mirrored toiletries cabinet in the bathroom, or a mirrored console in the hallway, for example. Mirrored furniture works best when used with care. Because of the special construction techniques necessary, the furniture

Above
When it's necessary to divide two spaces, but you don't want to block off light or the vista through the room, a thick sheet of coloured safety glass or acrylic is ideal for floor-to-ceiling sliding doors. Here, a small dining area can be made more intimate by closing the doors, while still giving a sense of the space behind.

or fitted across the entire wall. To prevent the mirror from steaming up, which is not only annoying but rather spoils the effect, you can buy thin demister pads that are stuck to the back of the mirror and wired into the lighting circuit.

Framed mirrors Mirrors in attractive frames act not only as space- and light-enhancers but also as decorative accessories in their own right. They can be hung almost anywhere, or even, if large enough, propped casually on the floor – a huge, gilt-framed mirror can work wonderfully like this. Framed mirrors can be made in a range of sizes and a variety of shapes, so it should be possible to find one that suits your purpose. What's more, these mirrors can be moved around whenever you need them somewhere else, or simply fancy a change.

The traditional place for a framed mirror, particularly in an older property, is over the fireplace. They are also useful in a hallway, on a bedroom wall, and over a bathroom washbasin.

Left
Accessories made from glass have a more ethereal air than solid objects. These slender vases in juicy colours have been grouped to make a simple but vibrant display.

Right
Mirrored furniture should be used judiciously but can have a stunning effect. This chest of drawers is versatile enough to be placed in a sitting room, and has an updated 1930s style so it is relatively subtle and discreet. In fact, you almost notice the reflections of its surroundings more than the piece itself.

Left
Instead of blocking off this mezzanine bedroom with a solid wall, glass provides a safety barrier but allows light into the upstairs space, and also maintains the feeling of soaring height downstairs.

Opposite
A spiral staircase has minimal impact, particularly when made from transparent materials. This sleek example uses glass treads, with a curving sheet of acrylic to support the handrail.

Using glass

You can use glass to open up a home and make it feel bigger. Glass allows more light in and spreads it around or, if you use obscured glass, filters and diffuses it while offering privacy (both visual and acoustic), or disguising unattractive views. At the same time glass increases a sense of space, either within a room by providing vistas from area to area, or through the entire property, or by offering a connection to the outside world. It works with both natural and artificial light, casting intriguing shadows and creating dramatic effects.

Glass can be used to replace many solid barriers, from walls and doors to furniture and fittings – even floors and stairs. Your main concern should be to fit the right type of glass in the right place. For any building projects it is advisable to consult an expert on the technicalities (such as load-bearing walls and safety glass), and to use a builder who has experience in such matters.

Types of glass The glass most commonly used around the home is known as "float" glass – because it is made by floating the molten glass on a shallow bath of liquid tin, producing a large sheet that is flat and distortion-free. Sheets of float glass can be as thin as 0.4mm ($^1/_{100}$in), or as thick as 2.5mm ($^1/_{10}$in), and may be clear, tinted, or coated. They may also be obscured with a texture on one side, or patterned with acid-etching or sandblasting, both of which produce varying levels of transparency.

Where glazed areas are large or especially vulnerable to breakage (such as in doors, shower screens, low windows, or glazed balustrades) safety glass is essential – and often a legal requirement. Safety glass is either toughened to up to five times stronger than ordinary float

tends to have a rather square and heavy form, so it is best to limit the number of pieces used, and to avoid anything that looks too monumental.

Mirror outdoors A highly effective way of increasing the sense of space in any small outside area is to add an expanse of mirror. Attach a sheet of mirror backed by safety glass to a wall or fence, or hang or prop (safely) a large framed mirror against it. The boundary will seem to disappear, doubling the apparent space, particularly if you can hide the edges of the mirror with foliage in the form of tall plants, or climbers scrambling up trellis on either side.

glass, or laminated by sandwiching a plastic film between two layers of glass. Some laminated glazing also offers protection against fire, as does wired glass, which has a fine steel mesh incorporated during manufacture. For certain applications, usually in a bathroom or toilet, it is possible to fit "smart" glass, which changes from clear to opaque when an electric current is passed through it. In other words, as you turn on the light with a switch, you can also turn "off" the glass so that no one can see in.

As an alternative to sheets of glass you can use glass blocks or bricks – these can be built into a wall in much the same way as ordinary bricks, though the wall must not be load-bearing. Obviously, the pattern of joins means that they create a completely different effect to that of a glass sheet, and this does also obstruct a small amount of light, but, on the other hand, a wall of glass blocks provides good insulation against both noise and heat loss. Blocks are available in a variety of shapes, colours, and textures, and can be built up straight or into interesting curves. Though most often found as shower screens or bathroom walls, they can also be used in stairwells and hallways, as insets in solid walls, or to create feature walls.

Glass as architecture It is sometimes the case that the most effective alterations to a home are the ones that cost the most and take up the most time and energy. Only you can decide whether you want to go for a quick fix or a long-term solution and all that it entails. That said, not all architectural interventions will necessarily bust your bank balance or take months out of your life – clever solutions may be possible that will dramatically improve your home in a relatively painless way. And, of course, if you are already renovating, rebuilding, or extending in some way, the following options could perhaps be integrated as part of the work without increasing your financial burden. Always ask advice from a relevant expert, perhaps a structural engineer, a structural glazier, or an architect, as some changes will require planning permission and/or building regulations, and may, if not properly carried out, have dangerous consequences for the structure of your property and your own safety.

For a marvellously light and dramatic effect, replace an entire interior wall with one made of glass, in the form of either a thick sheet of toughened glass or glass blocks. You could also create glazed piercings within a solid wall, along the top or bottom for privacy or centrally for eye-catching impact.

If you have plenty of light on one level but wish to increase the levels of light above or below, then consider installing a partial glass floor. It will act like an internal window, allowing light to travel up and down through the rooms. There are obvious structural and safety implications with this option – the glazing must be thick enough, and the steel, glass, or timber framework strong enough, to support its load – as well as ones for privacy, so you will need to choose the location with care and make sure that it is properly fitted by a professional who has experience in this area.

Finally, if you are adding a staircase (perhaps in an extension or a loft or basement conversion) or replacing an existing one, perhaps you can use glass instead of the more conventional timber. Glass can work well either for the whole structure or just for the risers or treads, which look great if lit from below and allow natural light into an under-stairs space. Open staircases made of glass are so minimal they seem hardly to exist, while spiral staircases look great when made from glass or acrylic. Both have the advantage of allowing light to pour from one floor to another. Alternatively, if you don't wish to go quite this far, it is relatively simple to replace a wooden balustrade with a glass or acrylic screen. This option can prove more safety-conscious than open balusters, and is striking to look at as well as light-enhancing.

Glass doors Replacing a solid door with one made of glass will create an instant transformation, allowing extra light to flow into an otherwise dark room while still blocking cold and draughts, separating spaces, and, if the glass is obscured in some way, offering whatever level of privacy is required. The size, style, colour, and arrangement of the door's glass panes will create a style and effect of their own, whether it is a thick, sliding panel of sandblasted glass with a contemporary look, or a vestibule door with stained glass inserts, which has a typical traditional appearance. If you are fond of the doors you already have, it may be possible to replace just the panels on them with glass ones, either clear or frosted.

The boldest step, and most expensive, would be to remove a solid exterior wall and replace it with a wall of sliding/folding glass doors. You

would have to consult a structural engineer and check with your planning authority as to whether permission is required, but the investment of time, effort, and money may well be paid back by the resulting effect of light flooding in and of opening up the space to the outside.

Transparent furniture and fittings A simple way to ensure that furnishings have as minimal an impact as possible on the space they occupy is to buy see-through pieces, made completely or partially from glass or acrylic, either clear or coloured. Free-standing pieces might include chairs, stools, desks, or tables, in various guises, whether coffee, dining, side, or console, with metal or wooden frames and legs. In style they can range from curvy, modern, minimal pieces to more traditional items that combine transparent or translucent materials with dark wood or wrought iron.

Fitted furniture made of glass could include wardrobe or cupboard doors that screen dust and dirt while allowing you to see the contents, perhaps clearly or through a pattern of texture or etching. In the kitchen or bathroom glass worksurfaces and splashbacks are hygienic, durable, and easy to clean, as well as good-looking. Glass has become a fashionable material for shower screens and enclosures, basins (especially free-standing hemispheres, which may be clear or coloured), and even baths. Glass shelving looks great in a bathroom, or elsewhere, though it does need regular cleaning in order to look its best.

See-through accessories It is possible to utilize glass and acrylic around the home in all sorts of ways, whether as functional pieces or decorative accessories or displays. Choose transparent lamp bases instead of solid ones, for example, or fit crystal finials at the end of curtain poles for a light, airy touch. Door and cupboard knobs and pulls may be made of glass or acrylic, as can light pulls and even switch plate covers. Displayed on shelves, vases and bowls made from glass will be more in keeping with a space-enhancing scheme than if they were made from an opaque material such as ceramic or wood, while discreet displays could consist of delicate glass objects such as perfume bottles or chandelier droplets.

Opposite
For maximum space and light this bathroom has a frosted glass door and a wall of glass blocks. Two large mirrors at the far end of the room also seem to enlarge the size of the whole area, while bouncing light around it.

Above
This bedroom features a combination of floor-to-ceiling mirrored and translucent doors. Their discreet styling adds to their space-making impact, and one of the mirrored doors is actually a cleverly hidden entrance to the interconnecting bathroom.

Windows

Even without undertaking major building works it will sometimes be possible – and not necessarily too costly – to increase the number and size of the windows in your house. And even if your windows are a fixed and permanent entity and altering them is not an option, you should easily be able to overhaul your window treatments to ensure that they offer privacy without blocking any light.

Making the most of windows

Until the making of flat panes of glass was mechanized about 150 years ago, large glazed windows were an expensive luxury. Medieval houses had tiny window apertures, often with no glazing at all, while 17th- and 18th-century homes were subject to a glass tax that deterred all but the very rich from installing expansive windows. However, in the 21st century not only is glazing relatively cheap, but technology has progressed to the point where it is easy to produce huge sheets of glass, held together with steel bolts, that blur the distinction between window and wall.

It is a simple equation: additional, bigger windows equal more light, more airiness, and an increased sense of space; fewer, smaller windows (or windows that have been covered with badly thought-out treatments) equal darker, gloomier, and more claustrophobic rooms. So,

Right
This pair of roller blinds is an unfussy alternative to ostentatious curtains, and complements the simple room scheme.

Opposite
A pair of large skylights over a kitchen work-surface allows daylight to flood through the room.

Left
A panel of sheer fabric
attached only to the lower
half of a window provides
privacy while allowing
diffused light through.
The utter simplicity of this
style makes it suitable for
any decorative scheme.

Opposite
A floor-to-ceiling,
wall-to-wall window is
the ultimate way to fill a
room with light and make
it seem more spacious,
but a bedroom needs
screening with something
unobtrusive. Here, a
white, louvred blind
is almost invisible, yet
does its job efficiently.

if you want to increase the sense of space and
the amount of light in your home you should look
carefully at windows – at whether it's possible
to install more of them or increase the size
of existing ones, and at how to make the
most of the windows you already have.

Adding or enlarging windows Professional
advice will be necessary from an architect or an
engineer, as altering walls and windows could
potentially adversely affect the structure of your
property. You'll also need to check whether you
need planning permission from the relevant
authorities, and ensure that new or replacement
windows meet building regulations and energy
efficiency requirements. The larger the window,
the more heat it will allow in and out, so it makes
sense to choose high-performance glazing
that controls heat gain and loss: ask a glazier
for glass with a low U-value and/or high R-value,
which indicates good insulation, either through
double or triple glazing or specially coated glass.

Skylights Roof windows, or skylights, are
startlingly effective in transforming a dark and
dreary space into a bright and airy environment.
Usually associated with loft conversions, they
can also be used for bathrooms, kitchens, home

offices, bedrooms, above a stairwell, or wherever
you have a space with a roof directly above.
Skylights can be fitted into flat as well as pitched
roofs, and can be installed singly, in pairs, or in
groups for a larger glazed area. In general, the
glazing should be equivalent to at least ten per
cent of the floor area in order to provide adequate
natural light, though nearer 20 per cent would
improve the overall effect. Larger windows may
be required in roofs with a low pitch in order to
maximize the outlook, and as well as size their
position is important – there may be technical
limitations, but as far as possible the windows
should be placed above the living area and with
regard to framing the view from both a sitting
and standing position. Of course, you must also
consider how the windows will look from outside,
and ensure that their proportions and position
relate to the building's overall appearance. It is
vital, too, to check with the planning authorities
that you are permitted to make changes to your
roof, and that any new skylights conform to
building regulations.

The simplest skylights are just fixed panes of
glass inserted into a roof's tiling structure, but for
more flexibility opening skylights are preferable,
allowing for ventilation and cleaning. These
may be top-hung or centre-pivoting, and can

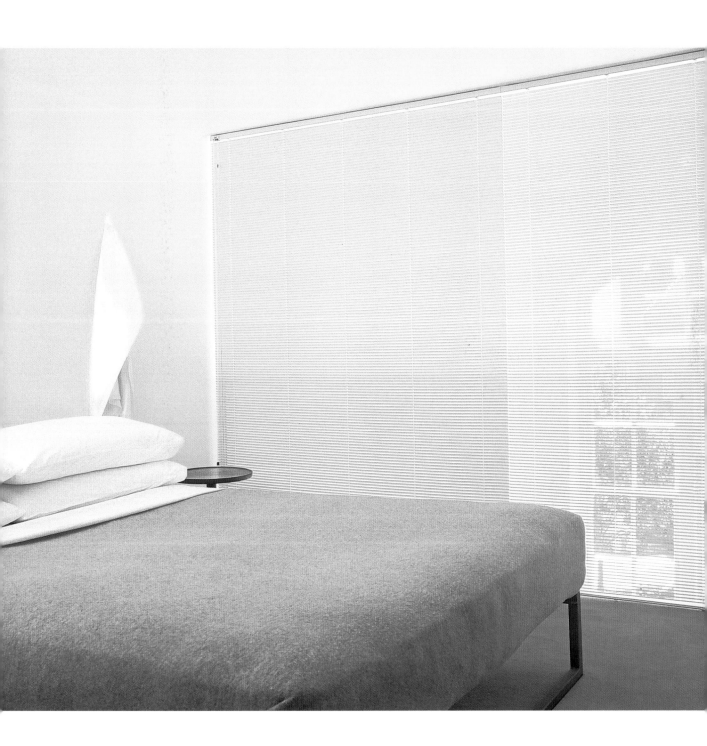

be operated by a rod, cord, switch on the wall, or by remote control. Some can even be opened by a smoke detector or closed by a rain sensor. It is also possible to install self-cleaning glass; this is coated with a special substance that reacts with daylight to break down dirt, which is then washed away when it rains.

The same factors that are important in energy-efficient windows are even more crucial with skylights, as heat loss or gain through windows on slanting roofs is much higher than it is through ordinary windows. For the best results, look for solar or heat-control glass, or energy-saving, low-emissivity glass.

If you are not allowed to install a normal skylight, it may be possible to fit a tubular skylight, or light pipe. This is a flexible tube with a highly reflective interior that connects a small, clear dome on the roof to an opening in the ceiling. Light is captured outside, redirected down the shaft, and then spread around the room with a diffuser, resulting in natural light in dark spaces. You can also add an electric light to the ceiling fitting to provide light when it is dark outside.

Plain and simple windows Convention has it that wherever we have a window we put up a curtain or blind. But why? Not all windows look onto public spaces where prying eyes might intrude upon our privacy, very few look out onto such ugly views that they have to be covered over, and it is rare for a room to be so glaringly bright that a curtain is required to make it dimmer. Sometimes it makes sense to ignore the usual custom and leave a window bare, thus allowing in the greatest possible amount of light, bringing attention to what is often an attractive architectural element, and avoiding any visual interference with the surrounding walls.

Where permanent screening is really necessary – perhaps in a bathroom or toilet, in a bedroom, or across the bottom half of a living room window, you may still be able to leave a window bare, simply by changing the type of glass from clear to patterned, textured, etched, sandblasted, tinted, stained, or otherwise obscured. Dimples, ripples, swirls, florals, abstracts, and other textures are available, which offer varying levels of translucency – though beware the rather dated look that such styles often have. For a more contemporary finish, solid panels of sandblasted glass look dramatic or, for a lighter feel, you could choose a sandblasted or etched pattern to suit the situation – perhaps spots, stripes, checks, or more traditional period designs. For the ultimate in hi-tech options, it is possible to maximize both light and privacy by using "smart" glass, which changes from clear to opaque at the flick of a switch. Do remember that if you are replacing glass in low windows, the bottom of a door, or some other situations, you should choose safety glass that does not shatter into dangerous slivers if broken. If, on the other hand, you don't want to replace the glass, it is possible to save money by creating a frosted effect yourself at home, either with a special spray (plus stencil), or a thin, stick-on film, both of which must be applied extremely carefully for a professional effect.

Minimal window treatments

Framing a window with curtains, obscuring it with a blind, or protecting it with shutters are traditional treatments that offer privacy, security, increased warmth, avoidance of the outside world, or, quite simply, make a good-looking addition to the room as a whole. As a decorative

Above
Hinged and folding wooden shutters are a simple and efficient way to screen a window. Painted the same colour as the walls, they blend in beautifully.

Opposite
Louvred wooden shutters are a versatile solution. They can be folded back neatly out of the way, closed completely, or the louvres can be adjusted to allow light in while still providing privacy.

Right
A plain wooden pole
is an unfussy choice.
The sheer curtains have
tab tops and a trimming
of ribbons to add
contemporary interest.

device window treatments provide, complement,
or augment colour, pattern, and texture, and
can give you an extra note of comfort and
individuality. However, clumsy window treatments
are a frequent culprit in making rooms appear
darker and more cluttered than they really are:
curtains that won't pull right back, blinds that
block light from the top of the glazing, and
loud patterns or bold colours that are visually
distracting and don't blend with the room's

overall scheme are all mistakes that can easily
be avoided. When selecting space- and light-
enhancing window treatments, it is best to
choose an option that is as minimal as possible
and that does its job without drawing too much
attention to itself. Where and how they will be
installed is the first consideration, as it can
sometimes be problematic to fit a curtain, blind,
or shutter that will cover a window when necessary
yet is also capable of being drawn, pulled, or

folded back right out of the way. Give plenty of thought to this question – if a pair of curtains won't work in the space allowed, it may be better to fit just a single curtain that pulls to one side, or a blind or shutters; where a conventional blind will be awkward you might consider an alternative such as a "bottom-up" blind or a screen (see p54). When there is more than one window in a room, it's best to stick to the same treatment all round, as any disparity of styles will only add visual confusion and clutter.

Getting the scale right is particularly important, too, as a small room will be dwarfed by curtains, shutters, or blinds that are too large, vividly patterned, or otherwise imposing. Material matters: your treatment should be made from a substance (perhaps wood or metal, fabric, or acrylic) that complements those used elsewhere in the room. And, in terms of style, it should be in keeping with the room's overall decorative scheme, whether sleek and modern, fashionable and fun, or soft and comfortable.

Shutters Shutters offer not only privacy but also extra security, and can be a great solution in a room that requires an unobtrusive window treatment. In a period property you may be lucky enough to have some installed already; if not, you can have them made to fit to your specifications. A pair of plain, full-length panels is the simplest option, but you may prefer to have them split across the centre like a stable door, constructed so they fold back in sections to fit neatly into a recess, or made with adjustable louvres. The traditional material is wood, which can be left bare or painted to match the walls so the shutters "disappear" into the background. However, for a more modern, funky look use panels of opaque white or coloured acrylic, fastened with slender

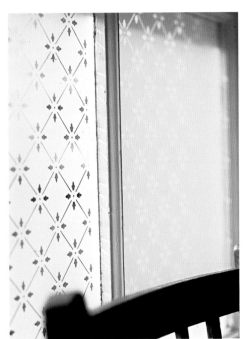

Above
Hang neutral linen curtains from bulldog clips suspended along a steel tension wire for a modern, minimal window treatment.

Left
Where permanent screening is required glass can be sandblasted or acid-etched, either plain or in an attractive pattern, as here.

Right
Tiny details such as
the pierced pattern
and the cut-out at
the bottom of these
blinds lift them from
banal to elegant.

Opposite
Dark wooden shutters
suit a traditional interior.
This one can be pushed
right out of the way to
let light fall through the
window in beautiful
patterns, or slid across
for a warm and cosy feel.

metal hinges. For a window in a flat wall (as opposed to a bay window) another alternative is a panel – perhaps of wood, acrylic, or even metal – that slides from side to side, either to cover the window or sit tidily next to it.

Blinds Tucked inconspicuously into the top of a window surround, blinds are ideal for allowing in as much light as possible when not in use. Because they are made with less fabric than gathered curtains, they tend also to be relatively inexpensive, and they are generally easy to install. In kitchens blinds are safer, too, as there is no flapping fabric that could get caught in the flames of a hob, while in the bathroom they can be made from water-resistant fabric. And for a bedroom you can back them with blackout fabric to ensure a good night's sleep.

Roller blinds are the simplest style – just pull down for privacy – but they can often be rather boring. To add decorative chic without compromising on subtlety, choose a plain, pale-coloured blind and add a bottom border in a contrast-coloured or textured fabric, with an interesting cut-out shape, or a pull that complements other materials in the room – perhaps a pebble, a leather knot, or a polished steel cylinder. There is no reason why a blind should not be made from two or more colours of fabric sewn together, as long as they are of similar weight. A practical way of using a roller blind at a window that requires screening at the bottom but not at the top is to use a blind made with a panel of opaque fabric combined with see-through mesh above, which lets light flood through. Another solution to this problem is to install a blind that pulls up from the bottom of the window and so only blocks out the area you want. If you would like to allow in more light when the blind is down, choose a sheer or a perforated fabric – this looks light, smart, and fashionable.

Deep, horizontally pleated Roman blinds are less utilitarian in appearance than roller blinds, and so tend to be used more often in bedrooms and living rooms. They are a good option for awkward window shapes such as bays, where a curtain could look large and heavy, and they can be made from all sorts of fabrics, from sheer to felt, linen to hessian – adding a touch of texture without being overpowering. They can

fall softly or crisply, depending on the fabric used and whether or not they are lined.

Less formal than Roman blinds, reefed blinds roll up from the bottom via a pair of cords. They don't necessarily align perfectly each time they're pulled up (this is part of their charm), but they are utterly simple and a prettier option than roller blinds. Pleated blinds, on the other hand, are very precise, and would suit a situation that calls for a minimal treatment.

If you would prefer to avoid fabric window treatments, an alternative to shutters would be Venetian blinds made of either wood or aluminium. Their great advantage is that their horizontal slats can be pivoted to control the light and amount of screening required. Discreet in appearance, metal Venetians are more contemporary, while wooden Venetians are classic and characterful.

Curtain styles Curtains block out prying eyes and make a room feel cosy at night but, as a general rule, the simpler the curtains the better. Heavy, dramatic swags, drapes, and tails, with

Above
Acrylic shutters are a funky, modern way to cover a window without obscuring the light or jarring with the architecture of the room.

Opposite
Startlingly effective in transforming a dark room into a bright and airy environment, skylights can also make a small, low-ceilinged room seem more generous in its proportions.

feature pelmets and grand tiebacks are a huge mistake – at best they are just too distracting and at worst they will block out light and make a room feel cluttered. Try to make the style of curtain work with the architecture, proportions, and style of the windows and their surroundings, rather than choosing fabric and headings in isolation. Sill-length curtains can make a window look short and stubby, while floor-length curtains emphasize a room's height; if you have space between the top of a window and the ceiling there's no need to hang the pole right above it - you could instead raise the pole so that the curtains elongate the room's proportions.

You can't really go wrong if you choose a simple track or pole hung with plain or subtly patterned fabric, as long as it is installed so that the curtains can be pulled right back away from the window when not in use. The less fabric you use, the lighter the curtain will seem – one-and-a-half times or twice the width of the window should be enough, and this could be pulled into gentle gathers or pencil-pleated for a smarter effect. If this seems too austere or dull, you can vary this basic style without creating an over-the-top, fussy window treatment. Instead of a plain heading, curtains could be tab-topped or made with tie headings, or have a wide hem that is threaded over a metal tube (though these options are often fiddly to pull). For a funky, contemporary look you can pierce large eyelet holes through which you thread a metal pole. Alternatively, the simplest of all curtains is a plain panel, hung from a track or pole, or – if you rarely want to draw it – with rings sewn to the two top corners that are hung from small hooks attached to the wall.

Simple curtains are best complemented by equally discreet fixings. Plastic or metal tracks are understated, cheap, and convenient, and useful for bay windows or other situations where it's not possible to fit a straight pole. However, they are not always terribly attractive, and may, if you wish, be hidden by plain wooden pelmets either painted or covered in fabric that matches the curtains. Poles, whether in wood or metal, should be free from fussy detailing, and finished with subtle finials that complement the overall décor of the room. These could be in the same material as the pole, or perhaps made from glass, mother-of-pearl, or wire-and-crystal. An alternative to the standard pole with curtain rings might be one made of bamboo, for a natural, rustic effect, or a tension wire fitted with tiny bulldog clips for a sophisticated, modern look.

Tiebacks are not really necessary when curtains hang beside a window, but are essential when they fall across it, as they allow the curtain to be pulled out of the way and so let in more light. The traditional tieback is made from the curtain fabric, with rings at each end that attach to a hook on the window frame or wall. A more up-to-date solution is a wooden or metal holdback shaped like a flattened C (resist the temptation to buy fancy shapes) into which you hook the fabric, or a slender post finished with a knob, behind which you can push the curtain.

Curtain fabric There is a great deal to be said for using inexpensive fabric in a scheme where space and light are essential. One-colour cotton or canvas, hessian or ticking, waistcoat lining or muslin, are all inexpensive but attractive, and are functional without undue ostentation. In many

schemes a plain, pale colour and an understated style is all you require. If you want to give definition and interest you can add a border made from a contrasting fabric, either down the vertical edge or across the bottom. If you can afford to invest a little more, look for interesting textures and unusual crossovers from the world of fashion in the form of, say, linen, felt, wool, mohair, men's suiting, saris, sailcloth, towelling, felt, denim, silk, or even cashmere.

When choosing fabric select a weight that is appropriate for the size of curtain, the room in which it is to be hung, and the job it must do – a sheer curtain in the bedroom will not work, for example, while a traditional damask will look odd in a modern setting, and a thick, heavy fabric won't hang well at a small window. Heavier fabrics tend to weigh down a room, while sheerer ones give it a more delicate, floaty feel, so choose material that is as light as possible. And if you come across a pretty tablecloth, a woollen blanket, or a fluffy sofa throw, they can all be adapted, as long as they are subtle and won't overpower the room.

Light

Indispensable on a practical level, light – both natural and artificial – also creates atmosphere, highlights and sculpts areas, and opens up spaces, influencing not just how you look at them but also how you feel about them. Light profoundly influences both ambience and mood, and there is no doubt that a light-filled home is not only brighter, but also more beautiful and harmonious too.

The importance of light

If you have ever felt that a room is boring, bland, or lifeless, but you can't quite work out what the problem is, it may well be the light that is at fault. No matter how beautiful the things it illuminates, poor lighting flattens and dulls, while clever lighting adds dynamism and interest, highlights colour, texture, and form, and can give "va-va voom" to the simplest of decorative schemes. Light is an incredible manipulator, and altering the light – whether it's enlarging a window or overhauling the electric fixtures and fittings – can be used to hide faults and illuminate good points, and ultimately to transform a home.

Light, whether natural or artificial, suggests, reveals, and delineates space: the better the light the better our sense and appreciation of a space. A small room may be just a small room, but with good light it can appear larger, more interesting, and more attractive. Lighting can also divide or unify spaces, creating two distinct areas in one room or harmoniously linking two separate areas; it can also be used to lead the eye from one space to another.

Designing with light is not always easy, but it's worth the effort to get it right. If successful, you can exploit the power of both daylight and electric light to create homes that are practical and good-looking, versatile and individual, and atmospheric at all times of the day and night.

Emphasizing natural light Natural light breathes life into your home, bringing different qualities to it throughout the course of the day, from stark morning light through to vivid afternoon light, soft twilight, and the darkness of the evening. Quite what character it offers will also be affected by the weather and the time of year, which means that sometimes the light will be soft and subtle, while at other times it will be precise and clear. Natural light is endlessly fascinating

Left
A stained glass door
provides privacy but
allows natural light
to flow from the bedroom
into the bathroom.

Above
A huge mirror reflects
the light that floods
in through the French
windows at the end of this
kitchen. White cabinets
and white-painted walls,
ceiling, and floor also
disseminate light, so the
room feels cool and airy.

Above
In a dual-aspect room such as this, it is very noticeable how much the movement of the sun alters the natural light. Wooden Venetian blinds are a classic choice as a means of diffusing bright sunlight.

and surprisingly versatile, and any artificial lighting scheme should be designed to complement as well as supplement the natural light already available in your home.

When assessing natural light observe the way it falls through external and internal windows, walls, skylights, and doors. In which rooms do you have more light in the morning or the evening? Ask yourself: is the light cool and northerly or warm and southerly? Is it even and bright, or dappled and moody? Work out where it is most prominent within each room, so that you can place furniture in appropriate places – perhaps a dining table and chairs by a sunny window or a desk beneath a skylight.

Though sometimes you may need to screen or block natural light with obscured glass or with window treatments, in general you will want to make the most of it, perhaps even by adding or enlarging windows, altering doors, or installing skylights (see Windows, p46).

Using artificial light Designing a well-thought-through lighting scheme is a highly effective way in which to enhance a sense of space. At night – or even during the day depending on the sources of natural light in your home – shadowy areas have the effect of making rooms look smaller, less inviting, and less attractive. This is particularly the case with what is, unfortunately, one of the most common forms of lighting in our homes – the central pendant. Too bright in the middle of the room, this usually results in dark corners and a blank, inflexible look. Too few lights placed around the room may result in the same problem, though it's not necessarily the quantity of lights that is the issue, but rather where they have been installed and the type of fitting or bulb.

You can bring light into dark corners either by increasing general light levels or by adding specific sources of light in different positions. You can also use light in sophisticated ways in order to disguise problem areas – by washing the long walls of a narrow room with light you may be able to make it appear less out of proportion, for example, or by installing a row of lights in a hallway you can lead the eye towards another room or an attractive view. Bouncing lights off walls and ceilings opens

them out, while decorative fittings can be employed as a feature in themselves.

It is best, if at all possible, to install fitted lighting during building works and before you have plastered your walls, laid your floors, and arranged your furniture. If you cannot do this, at least try to make it coincide with painting and decorating, so that installation work can be easily disguised. At the very least, without too much effort, you could re-angle lights, add free-standing lamps where required, and exchange switches for dimmers – so you can control light levels according to your requirements.

When planning your lighting start by analysing how each room is used, the amount of daylight it receives, its size and shape, any dark corners or special features, the layout of your furniture, and the effects you wish to create. Eventually, the types and amount of light sources required should start to emerge.

Below
The floor lamp in this room, ideally placed to illuminate a dark corner and to light a cosy evening's reading, is a subtle choice. Its slender metal base and simple paper shade are hardly noticeable among the brighter soft furnishings.

The professionals divide light into four main types, and it's likely that you will need at least one source of each per room. They are: general light, which gives good overall, background lighting; task lighting, to brightly illuminate a specific area such as a desk or reading corner; accent lighting, which highlights special features such as a painting or sculpture; and atmospheric lighting, which sets the mood, from a dramatic, theatrical mix of light and shade to mellow pools of light in different areas of the room.

There are a variety of ways to create each type of lighting. For general light, mix pendants with downlighters or spotlights on the ceiling (fixed to the surface or recessed), tracks, uplighters, and wall washers. For task lighting, the ideal source is an adjustable spotlight, either fixed to the ceiling or a wall, or in the form of a floor or table lamp. Accent lights might consist of ceiling spotlights, floor-level uplighters, wall-fixed uplighters, standard lamps, table lamps, and special shelf or display lighting. Atmospheric lights, on the other hand, can be more decorative in themselves, including any sort of light that creates interest and effect, even fires and candles.

It's worth noting that light is hugely affected by the type of bulb that is used in a fitting – not just its brightness but its quality, too. For instance, traditional tungsten is rather yellow, giving a warm and cosy effect. Halogen bulbs give a bright, white light and come as standard fittings or in low-voltage form; they are smaller than ordinary

Below
Inset ceiling spotlights can be used in any room. In this kitchen they simply disappear among the sleek fittings, yet provide excellent light by which to work.

Left
A row of lights
set at a low level
in a hallway leads
you through to the
inviting spaces beyond.

bulbs but they do require a bulky transformer. Fluorescent tubes are available in a range of shapes, sizes, and colours, and are useful in a variety of applications, though most often found in kitchens, utility rooms, and bathrooms.

This enormous choice of fixtures and fittings can make designing a lighting scheme, quite frankly, a bit overwhelming. However, if you take advice and do your homework the results can be amazing, and with some careful planning you can install a flexible and individual scheme that functions brilliantly, looks wonderful, and truly maximizes the potential of each room.

Light fittings The first principle of lighting a home is to remember that it isn't really about the fittings – your priority should be the light emitted: how it washes across walls, spotlights features,

creates intriguing shadows, and alters the whole mood of a room. But when the emphasis is on creating and maximizing space, it follows that it is even more important to choose fittings that are sleek and unobtrusive.

Recessed ceiling downlighters are ideal, as they give good overall light without intruding into the room itself. Make sure they are set back enough to avoid glare, and if necessary choose ones that are directional in order to highlight specific areas. It is also possible to recess lights into a wall, along a skirting board, into floors, up a staircase, or even within stairs themselves – though you'll need specialist advice before selecting and installing them.

Spotlights on cables or tracks is another option that is both versatile and discreet; these can often be fitted on ceilings, across walls,

around corners, and inside alcoves. As for pendants, there are hundreds of appealing styles that would provide attractive light while complementing a decorative scheme without overwhelming it – including glass or plastic globes or curvy cone shapes, tiny hemispheres on long arms, spun aluminium discs, or delicate stars. Even good old paper shades have lost their cheap, studenty look and now come in a variety of shapes, colours, and sizes; you could even string three or more together for subtle impact.

If you are fitting wall lights, look for examples that are slender and simple. Often the best solution is also the cheapest – for example, a plaster quarter-circle that you can paint the same shade as the walls. Alternatively, choose a fitting made from materials used elsewhere in the room (such as steel, wood or, plastic), to ensure visual cohesion.

The same applies to table and floor lamps. You will probably want these to form more of a feature in their own right, but it is still advisable to avoid oversized, bright, and fancy lamps that draw the eye to them rather than what they are illuminating. A simple slimline base in wood, metal, or glass, combined with a nicely proportioned shade in fabric or paper, would be a classic solution, or you could opt for a fashionable orb or cube made from acrylic or blown glass (white or coloured), which will glow with a gorgeous ambience.

Left
A glowing orb is one of the simplest options for a table lamp or floor lamp, providing beautiful light without drawing too much attention to itself.

Opposite
Create a glowing light, and a striking feature, with a light box. This one, simply an acrylic box with a light source inside, forms an unusual bedroom countertop.

Above
Lights recessed into the risers of steps or staircases are not only attractive, but also highly practical.

Ideas for living

Living rooms

For any living room, but particularly a small one, to be truly relaxing, beautiful, and practical, it must make careful use of every inch of space, and maximize light both day and night. Clever storage, well-chosen items of furniture, a suitable colour scheme, good lighting, and minimal, uncomplicated window treatments will all help to make this a room in which you will love to spend time.

Planning a living room

Before you even start to think about furnishings, you should consider how you use your living room. Is it primarily for relaxing with your feet up, or for more formal entertaining? Do children play in it or do pets sleep in it? Do you need to create space for a home office in one corner, for carrying out a hobby, or for special types of storage – perhaps musical instruments or a collection of some sort? You will need to work your lighting and furnishing schemes around these requirements.

You may also be able to improve the space by making relatively minor alterations. For example, if the door bumps into a sofa every time you open it, perhaps it could be re-hung the other way around, swapped for a sliding door, or removed entirely. If the radiator is in the way of a stretch of wall that could be used for storage, you may be able to move it. You might even consider installing underfloor heating, or slimline radiators that don't take up so much room. And a fireplace that's never used could be blocked up to create a useful wall against which you could push furniture, or it could be used as an extra storage space.

Once you have assessed the potential of your living room, you can start to develop a scheme that complements its architecture and layout, and in which all the basic elements work together to create a light, bright, and spacious room that feels comfortable and functions effortlessly.

Using colour, texture, and pattern To emphasize space in a living room it's best to have the walls a pale, plain colour – perhaps an off-white or a pastel. Doors, skirting boards, and window frames can be painted either the same or a slightly darker, complementary shade, while white is ideal for a ceiling as it seems to recede. If you love pattern and bolder colours you can introduce them in small doses – one wall covered in wallpaper, a vivid painting, a display of tinted glass vases, or an arrangement of cushions on

A cool and calm
atmosphere is created
in this living room by the
use of a greyish off-white
colour for the walls, floor,
and upholstery. The sheer
white blinds are so
minimal they are almost
invisible; they allow light
through while offering
complete privacy.

Above
You can use strong colours
as long as everything else
is laid-back and neutral.
These dramatic chairs and
the more traditional sofa
would be overwhelming
in a living room that had
too many other colours,
but are a great focal point
against the paler walls.

the sofa. On the floor, pale carpets are not practical, so you may want to introduce an understated pattern or lay rugs over floorboards. If the boards are in a light wood, painted a pale colour, or waxed so they have a glossy surface, so much the better.

By introducing a range of textures into a scheme that is otherwise relatively monochromatic you will add another dimension of interest. A deep-pile rug on polished boards is a great starting point, and you could choose sofas and chairs that are upholstered in textured fabrics, such as denim, velvet, corduroy, or bouclé wool. Cushions, curtains, lamp shades, and other accessories will add to the mix in order to create a gloriously sensual and liveable space.

Lighting for living rooms The first step in designing a lighting scheme for your living room is to introduce fittings that give good overall light – probably either a central pendant supplemented by lamps at floor and table height in corners and alcoves or, for a more modern look, a number of spotlights recessed into the ceiling. A dimmer switch will enable you to control the level of light and so create different moods. You may need to supplement this with bright lamps specifically placed for reading, working, or carrying out hobbies. If you have display areas, pictures, or attractive architectural features you wish to highlight, you could install spotlights, uplighters, downlighters, or special shelf or display lights to make the most of them. And, finally, you might want to add some form of atmospheric lighting, whether it be a lamp that casts a dramatic shadow or a mellow pool of light, or even firelight or candles for a warm, flickering, mesmerizing glow.

Window treatments This will depend largely on the architecture of the room. If you have a bay window in a period house, you may wish to install wooden shutters that fold back against the walls during the day, while if you have an offset picture window in a modern apartment you may want a huge sweep of voile that pushes back to one side. If a window has plenty of space above it will lend itself more to a Roman blind, while wall space either side might mean a conventional pair of curtains on a minimal pole or track works best. Consider what type of

treatment will maximize the light that comes into the room, while balancing your own need for privacy, cosiness, and, of course, to complement the décor elsewhere in the room. If you choose curtains or blinds, bear in mind that pale colours, subtle patterns, and floaty fabrics all help to maximize space, while attractive textures add interest to the overall scheme.

Choosing furniture The most important item of furniture in almost every living room is the sofa, and, as much as you need to make the most of the space, it's never worth buying a tiny sofa that is uncomfortable. That doesn't mean you need a bulky, deeply upholstered piece that seems to fill the whole room – a sofa with slimline upholstery, raised on legs so it seems to float, and in a pale, plain fabric, will still be comfortable but will not take up excess space and will look suitably minimal. The same applies to armchairs, though be wary of introducing too many spare items of seating – it may be that a pair of sofas (perhaps placed opposite each other), a modular or corner sofa, or a sofa plus some stacking stools is the best way to satisfy your needs.

Above
In what would otherwise be an awkward triangular space, here the built-in shelves, which can hold plenty of books, give this simple, functional room an interesting focal point.

Left

An entire wall of cupboards hides away all sorts of things that might otherwise clutter up this space. The glass coffee table is practically invisible, but is actually large enough to be extremely useful.

Opposite

When furniture can double as storage it helps reduce mess, as well as the amount of furnishings needed in each room. The light in the corner is a simple solution, providing atmospheric illumination after dark.

Coffee tables can also be problematic. If your coffee table eats up all the space in the middle of the living room, and blocks the way to switch off the TV or to draw the curtains, it might be better to put magazines and drinks in another place, such as a small table next to the sofa, a long, thin table behind it, or on a set of shelves or the top of a low bookcase. If a coffee table suits you best, find one that is slender and delicate in style, perhaps incorporating glass or another shiny or see-through material.

Try to restrict all other furniture to a bare minimum. Do you really need a table just to stand a lamp on, or could the lamp be wall-mounted? Is that magazine rack really necessary, or could you keep periodicals on a built-in bookshelf? Would a floor cushion be more space-saving than a chair? Question everything and keep only what is absolutely essential for comfort and practicality.

Storage solutions In any living room there will be things you want to hide and other items that you want to show off. A good scheme provides adequate storage space for all your clutter, such as CDs, DVDs, and videos, while allowing you to access items that you need on a regular basis, and space to display beautiful objects so that they enhance the room.

Work out just how much storage you need for which objects, whether any shelves or cupboards can conveniently be built-in (often the most satisfactory solution), and how many additional bookcases, tables, stands, boxes, and baskets you need to provide. In many living rooms shelves or cupboards either side of the chimney breast make ideal storage options. Alternatively, one all-encompassing solution may be the answer – an entire wall of cupboards, a shelf that runs the length of the room, or a huge sideboard or apothecary's chest. You may find furniture that can double as storage, such as a coffee table with a drawer, or a footstool that opens into a capacious box. Always look for storage that has maximum capacity with minimal impact, and that complements your decorative scheme, so that while working hard it also blends in beautifully.

Living room ideas

CLEVER PLANNING
Opening up the staircase has created room
for a banquette seat beneath. Instead of a
solid balustrade, a slim metal handrail and
tensioned wires allow light to flood through
both levels.

WELL-PLANNED LIGHTING
Lighting is a mixture of inset ceiling spotlights,
low-level lights up the staircase, and the
cheerful, flickering glow from the fireplace.

NEUTRAL COLOURS
The fundamental scheme of white and stone
is simple and light-enhancing, with touches
of more vivid colour to brighten up the room.

PLAIN AND SIMPLE
These chairs are comfortable but, like the
banquette and the coffee table, have clean,
simple, uncomplicated lines.

NEAT SOLUTION
There are no messy trailing wires here, as the music system has been integrated into the storage wall, with the tiny speakers hung high up out of the way.

TEXTURAL CONTRAST
Smooth surfaces and an emphasis on horizontal and vertical lines give this room a crisp, clean air, though softer textures have been introduced in the form of the nubbly stair-carpet, the fabric cushion-covers, and the carved wooden tribal figures.

ON DISPLAY
An inset display area adds interest and personality without overwhelming the room.

MODERN FIREPLACE
A "hole-in-the-wall" fireplace is unfussy and modern, and allows for an entire wall of built-in storage cupboards underneath.

Kitchens

Even in the smallest of spaces you can still have the kitchen of your dreams – a room that's a pleasure to cook in, is functional, and looks great too. It's all a question of the right approach. By combining ingenious, well-thought-out storage with space-saving appliances, really well-placed lighting, and carefully chosen materials, you should be able to enjoy both baking your cake and sitting down to eat it!

Planning a kitchen

In a small kitchen you'll want to make use of every possible inch of space, and what this comes down to is planning, planning, and more planning. Ideally, you should measure up the room and do a scaled drawing on graph paper, marking the positions of doors, windows, extractor outlets, sockets, and so on. Make scaled cut-outs of your appliances so that you can move them about on the drawing. Work out what cupboards, shelves, and drawers you'll need by listing all your food storage requirements and every bit of your kitchen kit, from saucepans right

down to the potato peeler. Allow space on worksurfaces for the gadgets you use regularly, ensuring there will be electrical sockets nearby, and find a home elsewhere for the ones you seldom use. Don't forget to leave room on the floor (perhaps tucked under a dining table) for any extras such as a pet's bed or children's toy box.

At the same time, consider how you use the room: cooking for one or for a family; regular entertaining; doing the laundry and/or ironing; homework; household admin, or as a part-time home office. These requirements will govern how much space should be devoted to which functions. Make lots of copies of your plan, then you can sketch out different configurations until you find the one that works best.

It is often easier to design a small kitchen than a large one, as there may be only one logical way in which you can set out the room. What's more, at least everything tends to be within easy reach – the trick is to avoid inconveniently sited appliances and corners that are either unused or awkwardly laid out. Smaller kitchens tend to be galley-shaped (a corridor, with either one or two long lines of units and appliances), L-shaped, or sometimes U-shaped. In a single galley kitchen, try to position the sink in the middle of the run; in a double galley it can be placed opposite the cooker for convenience. In an L-shaped kitchen the sink can be placed on one wall and cooker on the other, while in a U-shape you can choose where to place them – the aim, as far as possible, is to try to create what's called a "work triangle" between the sink, cooker, and fridge. Key pitfalls to avoid include putting appliances or drawers in corners, as they'll be difficult to open, and siting the hob next to a wall, high cabinet, or tall appliance, as it may scorch them. When it's even a squeeze to open conventional hinged cupboard doors, look for bi-fold, sliding, or roll-down doors.

If space seems impossibly tight, it is feasible to design or buy a tiny kitchen that fits neatly

behind sliding doors, or closes up like a large box – look for inspiration in the kitchens of yachts and boats, in offices, or in studio apartments. This is small-space living at its purest, with nothing more than a sink, drainer, and hob, a fridge, perhaps a slimline dishwasher, a wall cupboard, and a hanging rail. It will mean paring your belongings right down to the bare essentials, but it does prove that it is eminently possible to create a kitchen that works with maximum efficiency within the most minimal of measurements.

Fitted or unfitted? Fitted kitchens are designed to offer maximum storage, and are generally more efficient in their use of space than unfitted

kitchens. They can be installed to suit the dimensions of your room and to your personal requirements, but there is no getting away from the fact that they tend to look rather uniform, as they are almost inevitably built to standard dimensions. Unfitted kitchens, on the other hand, are charming and individual but are harder to plan, as you will have to find pieces that fit into the necessary spaces, are comfortable to work on, and that aren't visually jarring – quite a tall order.

If you like the sleek, clean look of a contemporary fitted kitchen this can be the ideal solution in a small space, as you can buy all the elements you need in one go, from pan drawers to dishwasher fronts. Try to avoid having too many

Left
Eye-level cupboards
tend to make a kitchen
feel claustrophobic but
they may be essential
for storage, so glass
fronts are a good idea.
These protect the
contents from splashes
and dust, but make
minimal impact.

Below
Careful planning prior
to installing a new
kitchen is vital. Work
out what you need
to store and what
you need to have
at hand, and ensure
that there are enough
electrical sockets for
all your kitchen gadgets.

high-level cupboards, as they tend to make the
room feel claustrophobic; if you really need the
storage space, either choose glass-fronted doors
or fit open shelves, crockery racks, or hanging
rails. Look for pieces on legs, rather than with a
solid plinth at the base, as this will really open up
the floor space. And if the materials you choose
for doors are transparent (glass or acrylic) or shiny
and reflective (such as glossy lacquer or stainless
steel), it will help to bounce light around the room.

For those who prefer the informal look
of an unfitted kitchen but can't afford to waste
any space, a good compromise is to mix a few
standard units with cupboards at different heights,
plus racks, rails, and shelves. Find pieces that
double-up in function, such as a small butcher's
block or trolley, preferably on wheels, which
provides a worksurface as well as storage space,
or a dining table on which you can also prepare
food. And avoid too many eclectic pieces, as
they can make the room look disorganized and
cluttered – aim for a certain unity of material,
size, and style, to provide some visual harmony.

Storage solutions Look up, down, and into the
corners to find room to stash away everything
you need in a tiny kitchen – use your ingenuity to
find just the right storage for you. One easy way
to get some off-the-peg solutions is to pore over
kitchen manufacturers' brochures. Their ideas are
tried and tested, from wire carousels that fit into
corner cupboards and revolve so that you can

easily access everything inside, to wall hanging systems from which you can suspend pans, plates, mugs, utensils, kitchen rolls, cook books, dish drainers, and baskets. Using the full height of a kitchen makes sense. If you are fitting eye-level cupboards extend them right to the ceiling, or if you have high ceilings you could suspend racks and rails underneath the cupboards on which to hang your more attractive utensils. By building the appropriate supports you can even wall-mount appliances such as tumble dryers or microwaves, thereby freeing up space for extra cupboards.

Alternatively, at just above floor level you may be able to fit drawers within the plinths at the base of your units, or slide flat cooking equipment underneath the oven. Shallow shelves can be fitted to the backs of cupboard doors to hold spices, cleaning equipment, or cutlery in tiny wire baskets, and slim, vertical drawers are ideal for holding jars, cans, bottles, and packets of food.

Right
Be inventive with
storage – it doesn't
have to be box-shaped.
This purpose-built
cabinet may be
expensive but it is
beautiful to look at.

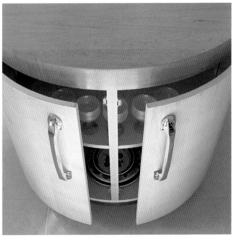

Appliances and fittings If you have a small
kitchen it makes sense to choose scaled-down
appliances. There are plenty of slimline versions
on the market, but before you buy you should
think carefully about how you will use them. Will
a small dishwasher's capacity be enough for your
family, and will you be able to fit your favourite
baking dishes into a small oven? There is no point
in saving a few inches of space if it's going to
cause huge inconvenience. Also ensure that the
appliances adhere to your visual scheme – if the
colours or styling clash, have fronts made that
match your cupboards so there's a flowing unity.

Fittings such as taps and door handles make
a great difference to the overall appearance of

Left
Small trolleys on wheels provide useful extra storage and food preparation areas, and can easily be pushed out of the way when not needed.

Below
Bold splashes of colour in this kitchen don't detract from the sense of airy brightness. White walls and a pale stone floor magnify the natural light, while wall-hung units and barely-there dining furniture maximize the floor area.

a kitchen, and in a small space you should aim for them to be sleek and slender, as visually unobtrusive as possible. They should be in character with the rest of the kitchen, avoiding fussy detailing and bright colours.

Using colour, texture, and pattern Most people's first thoughts about designing a kitchen are all to do with the style of the units, but in fact the walls, floor, and worksurfaces are the largest

areas of the room and so will make a huge impression. Aside from the practicalities of ensuring they are durable, water-resistant, and easy to clean, it is important to choose surfaces that help to enhance your space and maximize the light. Use pale colours with unobtrusive patterns (naturals such as the grain of wood or the patina of stone, or subtle, abstract, or organic prints), and combine a variety of gorgeous textures – perhaps adding wicker baskets to stone shelves, or a linen blind to a window above a ceramic sink.

A wooden floor that's either polished or painted a pale colour will really help to reflect light, as will glazed ceramic tiles, some vinyls, or a fashionable covering of rubber. On the walls, silk emulsion or kitchen paint (which is specially formulated to withstand damp conditions) is inexpensive and attractive. For splashbacks behind the sink and hob, you could choose ceramic tiles, stainless steel, glass, acrylic, or mosaic. Iridescent or mirror mosaic is particularly effective, and can be affordable when used over just a small area. Worksurfaces may be made from wood, stone, metal, laminates, man-made solid materials (such as Corian), or even concrete – try to choose something that is as glossy, smooth, and light in colour as possible.

Lighting for kitchens With knives, boiling water, and hot pans in the kitchen, good lighting is vital to allow you to see what you are doing safely, as well as illuminating the space in an airy, expansive way. For overall lighting, recessed ceiling spotlights are a good choice; alternatively use adjustable spotlights, or wall- or ceiling-mounted on a slender track. Low-voltage lights are smaller and neater in appearance, but you will need to find the space (perhaps in a ceiling void) to hide a bulky transformer.

The next priority is to illuminate the work-surfaces, hob, and sink, because if you rely on central ceiling fixtures alone you'll be standing in your own shadow. If you have wall cabinets or shelves you can mount lights on the bottom of them – either fluorescent or tungsten tubes or a row of tiny spots – hidden behind a baffle board so you see only the light and not its source. Simple downlighters can also be positioned in a recess at the base of a cabinet to function in the same way. Alternatively, use wall-mounted downlighters, preferably adjustable, or perhaps a series of extendable, hinged-arm lamps. Dangly pendants will interfere with the sense of space, though hanging a pair or trio of simple lights over an eating area is both good-looking and practical.

The kitchen/diner In a small home a separate dining room is a luxury, so you may have to use a corner of the kitchen for mealtimes. With attractive lighting you can make this area feel cosy and intimate in the evenings or bright and breezy for breakfast. Look for furniture that is not overly bulky or that, if necessary, can be folded, stacked, or hung up out of the way. A gate-leg, drop-leaf, or extending table may be the answer, or even one that folds down for use and flips up flat against the wall when not needed. Chairs should be comfortable but minimal, not overly bulky or padded (you can always put cushions on the seats). Avoid chairs with arms as they may not sit neatly under the table.

To create an informal dining area/breakfast bar you can simply extend a worktop so that there's room to fit your knees underneath. This approach works particularly well with a peninsular counter that makes an L-shape at one end of the room. Choose stools that are stable, have footrests, and that are easy to get on and off of.

Opposite
Despite its small size, the feel is big in this charming kitchen area. The palette of creamy colours and gentle mix of textures is comfortable and tactile, and the combination of open shelving and closed cupboards provides a good range of storage.

Above
This small island kitchen has plenty of well-organized space for storage and food preparation. Its monochrome colours and plain styling give it a timeless feel, and the natural light that floods through the large windows is well-controlled by louvred shutters.

Kitchen ideas

INTEGRATED APPLIANCES
Built-in appliances take up minimal space and
help create a feeling of seamless sophistication.

WALL-HUNG RADIATOR
Raising this off the floor makes the room
seem larger.

ISLAND UNIT
This combines a hob, storage, worksurface,
and breakfast bar in one neat unit.

SLIMLINE STOOLS
Slender legs and barely-there seats make
these a good choice.

GLASS SURFACES
See-through materials are ideal, and here thick slabs of glass have been used for the island worksurface, shelving, and even the extractor.

PALE WALLS
Walls painted with off-white emulsion are unfussy and increase the sense of space.

STAINLESS STEEL CUPBOARDS
A line of flat-fronted units, made from light-reflecting metal, has minimal impact but offers plenty of storage capacity.

WOODEN FLOOR
Polished, pale, and smooth flooring is ideal; this is practical, too.

Bedrooms

The most well-designed bedrooms are tranquil and restful, no matter what their size. In fact, small bedrooms can be warm and cosy yet still very functional. With a comfortable bed, good storage, and a flexible lighting system, you can create a room that is both well-organized and a pleasure to relax in – a room that will provide a calm and comfortable retreat from the world, both in the daytime and at night.

Planning a bedroom

To create a relaxing atmosphere you don't need a great deal of space so much as clever planning. Your first priority is to assess how you use the room: as well as sleeping, do you watch TV in it, listen to music, or chat on the phone? Or does the space double as a living room or home office during the day? Another important consideration is what you need to store in it – apart from clothes, shoes, and accessories, there may also be suitcases, hobby equipment, bedlinen, and other items. With these issues in mind you can decide how to arrange the space, perhaps with a screen to hide the computer, shelving for the CD player, or good lighting for reading and writing. Check that there is room in which to get dressed, to do things like drying your hair and putting on make-up, and to open all the doors and drawers.

If your bedroom feels claustrophobic, or just too full of clutter, it may be necessary to have a radical re-think of how space is allocated around the house. Perhaps a separate box room next door could become your wardrobe and dressing room. You may be able to find extra storage

Right
Two small rooms have been converted, by knocking down an interior wall, into a spacious bedroom with an adjacent wardrobe/dressing room. Recessed ceiling spots light both spaces inconspicuously.

space on a landing or under the stairs. Or, if you have high enough ceilings, it may be possible to build a raised sleeping platform, creating an extra "room", with space beneath for other activities.

Using colour, texture, and pattern These elements probably have a greater impact in the bedroom than in any other room in the home. For example, most people prefer to avoid strong colours as they are rather disturbing to sleep with. A palette of neutral colours such as stone, grey, chocolate, and ivory, or pastels from dusty pink to baby blue, are restful and relaxing. Patterns follow the same rules – anything too bold is unwise, but tiny florals, thin stripes, and organic abstracts can feel cocooning. In a small space it is usually best

to keep most of the room as a subtle, soothing backdrop, adding just one or two patterns, such as pretty wallpaper, carpet, or rugs, bedlinen, and curtains or blinds, for decorative softness.

Cosy textures are essential for comfort in the bedroom, and even with the plainest of colour palettes it's possible to layer texture upon texture to achieve a wonderfully snug feel. If you have wooden floorboards, for example, adding a deep-pile rug next to the bed not only feels delicious on the toes first thing in the morning, but also provides tactile contrast. At the window you might choose a combination of a sheer voile café curtain for privacy, with a heavy velvet or felt curtain (pulled well to the sides during the day) for warmth at night. And on the bed, you may

Above
Crisp white is elegant in a bedroom, and here it is nicely softened by a wooden floor and toning rug. Floaty voile at the window provides privacy and also textural contrast to the cotton sheets, quilted bedcover, and painted-wood shelving.

choose simply a plain cotton duvet cover that's
edged with a fine trim of lace or piqué, or layer a
crisp cotton or linen sheet with a ribbed woollen
blanket and a pair of mohair and satin cushions.

Lighting for bedrooms It is best to avoid glaring,
unflattering lights, but you'll still need good
general illumination for getting dressed, and
specific lighting for activities such as reading or
putting on make-up. It can be tricky to get just
the right mix of general ambience, clear, bright
light, and romantic moodiness. And even in the
bedroom, where the impression of dark corners is
not so much of a problem as it is elsewhere, you'll
still want to use lighting to maximize your space.

If your bedroom ceiling is relatively low avoid
having a dangling central pendant – though if
there's room to hang one, a delicate chandelier
can give the right boudoir feel. Recessed
spotlights provide a neater look, and can be
supplemented by pretty wall lights. For the most
flexible general lighting, put them all on a dimmer
switch so you can control how bright the room

is at all times of the day and night. Extra lights
should be added near a mirror and beside the
bed, each with its own switch. Rather than taking
up space on the floor or side table, these lights
can be mounted on the wall (make sure they're at
exactly the right height) and should be adjustable
so you can direct the light to wherever it's needed.

Choosing furniture However small your bedroom,
don't compromise on the size of your bed – the
wider the better to avoid disturbance from your
partner (especially if you have children who
like to creep in too) – and it's best if it's about
10–15cm (4–6in) longer than the taller person.
Look for styles that are raised on legs – either a
traditional wood or metal bedstead or a simple
wooden platform. You can store things underneath,
but make sure they're pushed right to the centre
so you can't see them – otherwise the impression
of extra floor space will be ruined. The more
slender the bed frame the less dominant it will
appear – so a "sleigh" bed is not a good option,
though a delicate four-poster could work really

well (see p34). And although you'll need a head-board for leaning against when reading, avoid a footboard, which takes up unnecessary space.

For occasional use in a small spare bedroom you could have a sofa bed, a roll-out bed (a single bed with another underneath), bunk beds (best for children only, though), a roll-up futon, or even a good-quality inflatable bed.

In a small bedroom there won't be room for much other furniture except for essential storage (see below), so you'll need to think laterally. Instead of a dressing table, could you use a slim shelf, with make-up kept in a neat row of baskets and a mirror propped or hung up next to them? If you need a seat, could you use a blanket box with a cushion on top? And instead of bedside tables, how about mounting lights on the wall and putting up a small, semi-circular shelf below for your alarm clock and a book? If you have a TV, radio, or music system in the bedroom, try to wall-mount these, too.

As well as keeping furniture to a minimum, look for pieces that make as little impact on your space as possible. Choose items that are slender in form, small (as far as is practical) in size, and either pale in colour, or, perhaps, reflective (mirrored or ultra-shiny) or translucent (made from glass, acrylic, or wire). They could also be foldable, on castors, or able to be hung or stacked out of the way.

Storage solutions Wardrobes, chests of drawers, blanket boxes, and other bedroom storage tend to be big and bulky – and sometimes there is no getting around this. Once you have pared down your clothing and assessed whether you can store out-of-season clothes in another room, or use a separate space as a wardrobe/dressing area, you may still be left with a large number of things to store and not much room to put them in.

One solution is to build an entire wall of storage, which will hold masses of stuff and, painted the same colour as the other walls

with minimal handles or invisible push catches, will disappear into the background without seeming to eat into your space. Built-in storage can make use of otherwise redundant areas, such as the triangles created by sloping ceilings or the recesses either side of a chimney breast, and can be tailored to suit your requirements exactly.

If, on the other hand, you can't afford custom-built furniture or you prefer the eclectic look of free-standing pieces, there are various ways to get more storage for less visual impact. First, choose taller, thinner pieces, such as a wardrobe that reaches right up to the ceiling, or a tallboy rather than a chest of drawers. Look for storage that works really hard, perhaps on castors so it can roll under the bed or into a recess when not in use, or that doubles as seating or a table. In a really tiny room, for example, you could build the bed up so that the entire base consists of drawers, lean a bamboo ladder against the wall for hanging skirts, trousers, and dresses on, or hang a shoe tidy from a hook on the back of the door.

Whatever storage you have, ensure you get the most from it by modifying it where necessary – adding an extra rail if you only hang short items in a wardrobe, for example, or screwing small hooks inside the doors to hold belts, scarves, and bags.

Window treatments During the daytime it's lovely to be able to walk into a bright and airy bedroom and throw open the windows, feeling clean air freshening up the room. So make sure that curtains, blinds, or shutters don't block out the sunshine through being badly positioned.

However, at night the opposite is the case, and for warmth, privacy, and to keep the early morning sun from waking you, you'll probably want to cover the windows really well. Unless you've chosen shutters or wooden louvre blinds, this is an opportunity to add softness to the room. Both Roman and roller blinds are neat and unfussy, and can be given a decorative flourish with the addition of a contrast border, a trim, or an interesting pull. Otherwise, simple curtains in an appealing fabric are ideal for dressing the room. Heavy fabrics are warm and sensuous but should be minimal in style, while with lighter fabrics you can afford to be more indulgent, gathering them into romantic frills but avoiding outdated swags that would clutter up the window.

Left
The fitted wardrobes in this bedroom provide a wall of mirrors that serve to double the apparent size of the room.

Opposite
In a loft-style live/work apartment, the bed has been fitted behind a pair of folding doors that are used to separate the space at night.

Bedroom ideas

SIMPLE WINDOWS
A white roller blind provides privacy but
blocks out very little light and complements
the unfussy decorative scheme.

SOOTHING COLOURS
A colour palette of gentle white and
creams, together with natural wood,
is subtle, calm, and restful.

INCONSPICUOUS STORAGE
Raised off the floor and painted cream so as
to appear less bulky, the storage cupboards
have been built around the window so that
they don't obscure any light.

MOVABLE BED
The bed is on castors, which means that not
only does it seem less bulky than a divan,
but it can also be moved easily if necessary.

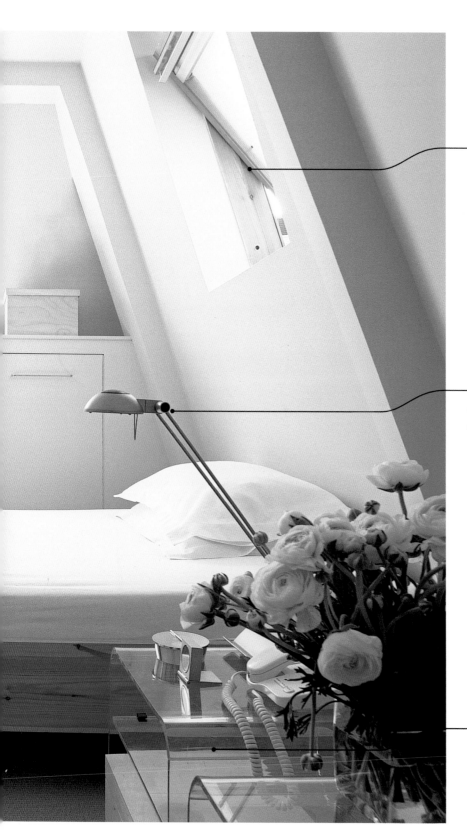

LETTING IN LIGHT
Adding a skylight window is not particularly expensive or difficult, but massively increases the amount of light in the room.

FLEXIBLE LIGHTING
This reading light is a great choice: slender but adjustable and bright. It can be pulled over the bed or pushed out of the way when not in use.

STREAMLINED FURNITURE
Slimline acrylic furniture is utterly minimal in impact and works well in a contemporary bedroom.

Bathrooms

These days we demand more from our bathrooms. Primarily we need them to be a functional, efficient place in which to keep ourselves clean; but we also want the bathroom to be a kind of sanctuary – an indulgent, luxurious room in which to unwind and de-stress. Fortunately, with good planning and just a little ingenuity and inspiration, it's possible to create a room that will live up to these great expectations, even in the tiniest of spaces.

Planning a bathroom

As with kitchens, it can sometimes be easier to design a small bathroom than a larger one. Once you have worked out what fittings you want, there may be only a limited range of possible locations for them, so you don't have to worry about where things will go, just how to make them function as efficiently as possible without sacrificing comfort and good looks. If you do want to change things around from the present arrangement, bear in mind that, while more or less anything is possible, moving the soil stack, the water pipes, the extractor fan, or even a radiator will all add to the cost.

Good planning is vital for any bathroom, as mistakes will be both difficult and costly to rectify later. First, look at the big picture – should you knock a wall down so that you have one large room instead of a pokey bathroom and tiny, separate toilet? Can a toilet be fitted under the stairs, freeing up space for a generously sized roll-top in the bathroom? Do you need a double basin so that you and your partner can brush your teeth at the same time in the morning? Could you make do with just a shower, and no bath at all?

When you are really short on space a bathroom can be fitted into the corner of a loft, one end of a large bedroom, or simply any space that is long enough for a bath or high enough for a shower. However, do allow knee and elbow room around the lavatory and basin, and space in which to dry yourself next to the bath and shower. Unless you install underfloor heating, you will need wall space for a radiator; also make sure you allow storage for cleaning equipment and bathroom necessities. The best way to ensure that your design will work is to draw up a scale plan on graph paper, and make full-sized paper cut-outs of each fixture that you can move around the roomplan.

Using colour, texture, and pattern Unless you want to make a very bold statement it is best to avoid coloured bathroom suites. However, on

Left
A limited palette of colours and materials, together with simple, clean lines, a large, unfussy mirror, and wall-mounted taps all help to make this room appear airy and spacious.

Opposite
A radiator that doubles as a towel rail saves space elsewhere (and is conveniently situated over the bath), while an extra-wide ledge around the bath provides room for the necessary toiletries.

walls, floors, worksurfaces, and splashbacks you can introduce gorgeous textures in the form of luxurious materials, which, as you only need them in small quantities, are affordable for a small bathroom. Think of a background of exotically grained wood, mosaic, marble, terrazzo, limestone, or slate, with leather storage boxes, linen blinds, and waffle towels. By choosing tactile surfaces you can avoid the common mistake of the too-clinical, all-ceramic bathroom.

Maintaining a neutral colour palette will automatically open up a small bathroom, giving it a clean and sophisticated, contemporary feel. If you can't live without colour, watery blues and greens have that cool, clear quality that will still make the room feel light and airy.

Lighting for bathrooms In a small bathroom light fittings are likely to be close to areas that get splashed, so for safety's sake it's vital to check with a qualified electrician what types of fittings you can install where – you may have to use ones with a waterproof rating. This means that a decorative chandelier may be out – though in fact any lights that dangle or protrude too obviously are inadvisable from an aesthetic point of view anyway, as they will interrupt the impression of smooth-flowing space. Instead, choose recessed ceiling spotlights, or neat directional lights mounted on a slender ceiling- or wall-track. As a hidden light source you could fit strips of lights beneath wall units (with a baffle board in front to avoid glare), or behind a splashback, or even (fully protected) behind a coloured acrylic bath panel, so that the bath gives off a fascinating glow. You should also illuminate the mirror above a basin really well, perhaps by using a pair of slim, wall-mounted lights, one on either side.

Try to create a bathroom lighting scheme that suits all your requirements, from putting on make-up on a dark winter's morning to reading in the bath. This may be achieved simply by fitting a dimmer switch, or it may be a more complex arrangement of two circuits, one for working lights and the other for more ambient lighting.

Reflective and transparent materials It is easy to follow the space-making rule of using as many reflective and transparent materials as possible, as almost all bathrooms automatically consist

mostly of hard, shiny surfaces. A conventional bathroom will have ceramic fittings with a vinyl, linoleum, or cork floor, and tiled walls. A more contemporary look can help maximize the space even further with a greater range of see-through and light-enhancing materials. Glass is great for basins, shower doors and screens, shelves, and cupboard doors – it is even possible to find glass baths. Another advantage of glass is that it looks great when lit up; the disadvantage is that you do have to work quite hard to keep it clean. Translucent acrylic, too, can be used for shelving, splashbacks, bath panels, and cupboard doors. If you like the utilitarian look you could fit a stainless-steel bath and basin, or use that material for wall or bath panelling; for a softer approach you might prefer the lustre of iridescent mosaic. On the floor you could fit shiny tiles or a sheet of rubber, or perhaps paint an existing wooden floor with glossy marine paint in a pale colour. Finally, include

Above
To optimize space use glass and mirror as much as possible. This stretch of mirror is actually the front of an entire wall of storage cabinets.

Opposite
This tiny room contains a toilet, basin, and shower – but good lighting, and the fact that the basin is wall-mounted and the shower is enclosed by a clear panel of glass, makes the most of the limited space.

as much mirror as possible, whether framed or as wall-to-wall sheeting, in order to reflect and magnify both natural and artificial light.

Window treatments While it is always nice to have a large window in a bathroom, there is very often a trade-off between letting in as much natural light as possible and maintaining a decent amount of privacy. If your bathroom is not over-looked you don't have a problem, but if the neighbours can see in, you will require some sort of screening. A good solution is to use etched, opaque, or coloured glass in the window itself – or perhaps in the bottom half only, which will still allow you to see the sky while lying in the bath. A neat blind is a nice alternative – choose either a roller or a Roman blind that tucks into the top of the window frame without obscuring any glass when it is not in use. If you need to have the blind pulled down permanently, you could consider either a "bottom-up" version, or one made from solid fabric at the bottom and see-through mesh at the top. (That way you can conceal what's necessary and still let light in through the upper portion of the window.) Shutters are an option – you could choose the traditional look in wood, or a cool and contemporary version made from sheets of acrylic.

Curtains in a bathroom can make a pleasantly soft contrast to the hard surfaces elsewhere. However, it is best to be restrained: floaty sheers in simple gathers are a better bet than dark, heavy fabrics for lightening up the space. A modern version of the net curtain might work well – a café curtain hung across the bottom half of the window only, in the form of a flat panel of muslin, threaded over a simple wire.

Choosing a suite Bathroom manufacturers have done an admirable job recently in designing fixtures that will suit even the smallest of rooms, and there is now plenty of choice that does not compromise on either function or looks.

When you would like both a bath and a shower, but haven't quite got the space to fit them in, the answer is a shower-bath, where one end of the bath bulges out to create a generously rounded space in which to stand up. Unlike old-fashioned showers over baths, which are cramped and, with flapping shower curtains,

sometimes leaky, these are comfortable to use and have custom-fitted, curved glass screens to make them watertight. If you love bathing but don't have room for a standard-sized bath, the options include shorter baths, deep-seated square baths, or perhaps a corner bath. However, it may make sense to get rid of the bath entirely, and simply install a luxurious shower.

As basins are available in so many shapes and sizes, it should be no problem to find one that suits your room. If it comes with a towel rail beneath you will save space on the wall that you might otherwise have had to use for a towel ring or hook. Wall-mounting the taps makes for a cleaner look. Do check that a very small basin has a corner to hold soap – some don't, in which case you would have to add a wall-mounted dispenser. Toilets, too, come in space-saving designs, and in a tight spot you could fit a corner loo or one that is angled to make it fit more easily into the configuration of the room.

Even without using smaller-than-average or ingeniously shaped fittings, it is possible to make a bathroom appear more spacious than it really is. One way is to install a wall-mounted basin, toilet, and, if you want one, bidet. Not only do they look swish and sophisticated, they also free up floor space beneath, so the room appears larger.

Above
Bold colour has been
used to make a dramatic
impact without detracting
from the space, thanks to
a background of neutral
tones and careful use of
plain materials, fitted in
precise, horizontal lines.

Free-standing baths, whether a traditional roll-top or its modern equivalent, may be huge, but have the same effect. Toilets can be made to look more minimal by hiding the cistern behind a false wall (these are called "back-to-wall" toilets). And showers appear sleeker with a simple glass screen rather than a patterned curtain.

Storage solutions When space is really tight it is tempting to avoid building cupboards as it might seem that they will just take up too much floor area. However, fitting well-designed storage is often a good way of gaining extra space, particularly in a bathroom, as there are so many necessary but unattractive things for which you'll

need to find a home. And because cleaning products, shampoos, cotton wool, make-up, and so on are pretty small, you will not require huge cabinets, just slimline ones that can be squeezed into spare corners almost unnoticeably.

If you are overhauling an entire bathroom, this is your chance to hide shallow cupboards within wall panelling. If you are fitting tongue-and-groove, for example, make it project from the wall a little further than normal and not only will it hide the pipework but you will also be able to put up shelves within it. Add doors at strategic positions and you have cupboards all around the room, as well as a handy shelf on top. Alternatively, punch holes in false walls to make niches in which to keep toiletries, particularly next to the shower and bath. And look for other places where small cupboards could be added – perhaps above the toilet or bath, around a basin (you could buy a ready-made vanity unit), above the door, or beside the shower. Paint them the same colour as the walls and they will all but disappear, or front them with mirrored doors and they will reflect light around the room. If you are really stuck, you could replace the bath panel with one that has magnetic catches, and use the space around and under the bath for storing bits and pieces.

If you cannot fit custom-built storage, or prefer the more eclectic look of free-standing pieces, choose from chests, cupboards, boxes, and baskets made from materials that will co-ordinate with the rest of the room, such as wood, leather, wicker, plastic, chrome, acrylic, or mirror. Try to find pieces that fit really well into the space, perhaps pushed under a basin, tucked into a corner, or stood in neat rows along a shelf.

When you want to put things on show there are plenty of options, from glass shelves to radiators that double as heated towel racks, over-door hooks to chrome or coloured-plastic trolleys. For the shower you can fit small shelves, soap dishes, or baskets on suckers (make sure the suction is strong enough), or extendable poles that fit into a corner and have integral shelving. A conventional bath rack is handy when balanced across a bath, and could be in traditional brass or more contemporary bamboo. And next to a basin, or on a window ledge, you might choose a set of glass or acrylic pots to hold attractive accessories.

Below
Neat, wall-mounted fittings, a neutral colour palette, and good use of glass and mirror make this compact space feel light and airy.

Left

Good storage ideas are
by no means restricted
to sleek, built-in units.
Here a softer, more
feminine look has been
achieved by the clever
device of a shelf for
storing toiletries fronted
by a gilded mirror.

Above

Natural light floods into
this bathroom through the
top half of the window; the
bottom half is screened by
opaque glass for privacy.
The warm, creamy tones
and a general lack of
clutter make it a calm
and restful room.

Bathroom ideas

MIRRORED STORAGE
Capacious floor-to-ceiling storage has been
fronted with mirror, thus providing plenty of
room to hide clutter while at the same time
doubling the sense of space.

STREAMLINED SANITARYWARE
The simple basin, made from translucent
glass, has minimal impact.

SLIMLINE FITTINGS
A slimline cupboard tucked under the basin
makes the most of unused space, and is just
large enough to hold everyday essentials.

NATURAL FLOORING
A smooth, pale, plain stone floor reflects
light from above and adds to the feeling of airy
openness.

OPEN SHELVING
A good option for storage is to mix streamlined cupboards with open shelving on which to display carefully chosen objects.

UTILIZING WALL SPACE
When the floor area is limited make the most of walls instead. It may be narrow, but this tall cupboard can hold plenty of cosmetics.

PAINTED WALL SURFACES
Pale, matt-painted walls reflect light without looking clinical.

SUSPENDED TOILET
A wall-hung toilet appears almost to float, and frees up the floor space so that the room will seem bigger.

Home offices

Whether you run a small business from your home or simply require an occasional surface for a laptop, sketch book, or notepad, it's important to ensure that your home office really works for you. Not only must it be completely functional, but it should also fit into your home seamlessly, without robbing you of space, and there's no reason why it shouldn't also complement perfectly your decorative scheme.

Planning a home office

When setting up an office in a small home, the main problem is where to put it. How much space you devote to it very much depends on the nature of your work, whether you need special facilities or equipment that requires extra floor space, and whether you receive visitors or host meetings. You may not have the luxury of a dedicated room, but can you convert a loft or a basement, double up in a dining room or bedroom, or squeeze a work space under the stairs? Alternatively, have you got the necessary ceiling height to add a mezzanine level above another room, or build a work platform at the top of the stairs? Perhaps you could even use a well-lit and heated garage or garden shed?

If you work alone, with just a computer for company, you can squeeze an entire office into quite a small, otherwise redundant space. As long as there's room for a worktop and a chair, you can fit storage boxes under the desk and hang shelves on nearby walls, creating a compact work station where everything is easily to hand. However, if you need to use the corner of a living room, kitchen, or bedroom then plan ways to minimize the disruption to both activities. Rather than clearing your work out of the way at the end of every day, for example, organize things so that you can push the desk into a corner, pull a screen or curtain in front of it, or roll your files out of the way. A room divider with shelving on the office side will provide both storage space and privacy. The alternative is to design, or buy, a completely self-contained, ready-made office-in-a-box.

Lighting for home offices If you have fantastic natural light this is one case where it can actually be detrimental: coming from either directly in front or right behind, too much light plays havoc with the visibility of a computer screen. Positioning the screen at 90 degrees to the light source should help, or you may have to fit blinds or curtains to

Above
If you are using part of a room as a home office, then a sliding, frosted-glass door is a brilliant way of making it all but disappear when not in use, without seeming to block off the space entirely.

Opposite
A sturdy table built across an entire alcove makes the best use of space, while a narrow strip light hanging above provides good illumination. The Roman blind is attractive but functional, while the pale colour scheme makes the room feel pleasantly bright.

Above
A multi-level desk provides a lot of working area in one small space. This combination of metal and glass makes minimal impact, and the castors mean it can even be pushed out of the way when not in use.

filter the light so that you can see properly. However, too dark an office is equally undesirable, and home office lighting needs to be bright, though not glaring. Overhead lamps or spotlights, recessed into the ceiling or on tracks, and preferably directional, are ideal, and you may also need to supplement them with a fully adjustable desk lamp or wall-mounted lamps.

Storage solutions List all your office paraphernalia, and think about how it can best be accommodated to be close to hand without causing clutter. A floor-to-ceiling, fitted cupboard may well be the answer, with shelves set at different heights to accommodate your accessories. Alternatively, open shelves will be less expensive to install but will only look tidy if you buy co-ordinating boxes, trays, and holders in which to keep everything. Free-standing storage is another option. Use the walls as much as possible – blackboards and pinboards are incredibly useful, as are wall systems that hold hooks, small baskets, and sundry bits and pieces.

Choosing furniture All that most people really need in their home office, apart from well-designed storage and adequate lighting, electrical sockets, and a phone line, is a sturdy desk that's big enough for their work and set at the right height (ideally around elbow height), and a comfortable chair. To make the most of your space you could opt for a desk fitted across a corner or built to your exact size requirements. It doesn't have to be made from wood – a sheet of toughened glass is nicely minimal, while whiteboard is useful for jotting down telephone numbers, and boxes, cupboards, filing drawers, and wastepaper bins can all be accommodated underneath. A multi-level desk, with a pull-out tray on which to put your keyboard and a lower shelf for the printer, gives plenty of surface area.

Finally, your chair should be as much of an investment as you can afford. Don't sit all day on a fold-up chair, a stool, or a dining chair – it may save space but could result in a visit to the osteopath. Instead, choose a stable, height-adjustable office chair with a five-point base and, above all, good back support. With so much choice available, you should easily find one that blends in with its surroundings.

Above
Tall, glass-fronted
cupboards provide
ample, well-organized
storage here, while the
leopardskin-upholstered
office chair is fun
and personal but also
practical. The roller blind
is essential for filtering
the light, but does not
impose on the room.

Home office ideas

SIMPLE WINDOW DRESSING
The simple and minimal metal louvred blind
has an air of efficiency, and can be adjusted
to filter the light.

PRACTICAL ACCESSORIES
A magnetic memo board is practical and
unfussy, and useful for displaying inspirational
images, notes, lists of deadlines, or
telephone numbers.

ADJUSTABLE LIGHTING
The desk lights are fully adjustable to provide
illumination exactly where it is needed.

SPLASH OF COLOUR
Funky chairs add a joyful note of colour
to an otherwise understated white room.

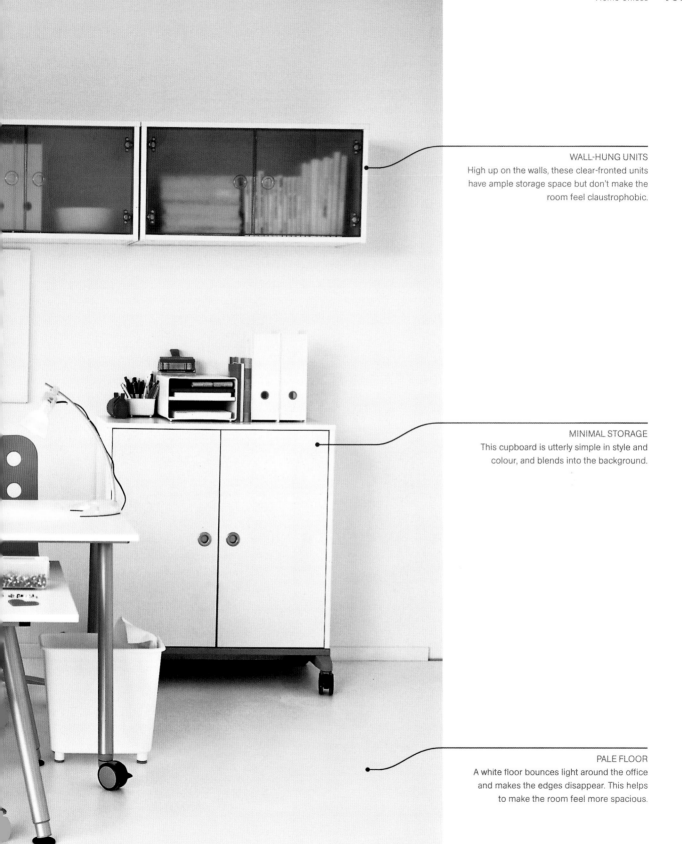

WALL-HUNG UNITS
High up on the walls, these clear-fronted units
have ample storage space but don't make the
room feel claustrophobic.

MINIMAL STORAGE
This cupboard is utterly simple in style and
colour, and blends into the background.

PALE FLOOR
A white floor bounces light around the office
and makes the edges disappear. This helps
to make the room feel more spacious.

Outside spaces

It might be just a courtyard, a balcony, a roof terrace, or a tiny patio, but any sort of outside space, however small, can be treated as an integral part of your home. And if you make the most of the space you've got, you will not only have increased the useable floor area of your home, but also created somewhere to grow plants, get a breath of fresh air, relax outside on a summer's day, and entertain friends.

Planning your outside space

Connecting your interior to the outside world will make both areas look bigger. A view from one side of the living room to the further end of the outside space beyond will make the room seem twice the size, so maximize the potential of these views by using minimal window treatments and not placing furniture in the way. You may even want to investigate the possibility of turning a window into a doorway, or installing sliding or folding glass doors to replace an entire exterior wall.

As for the outside space itself, if possible try to use materials and colours that continue the theme of your interior. Imagine that you are designing two adjacent rooms rather than an inside room and a garden, and aim for decorative coherence rather than jarring contrast. Choose fences, walls, and flooring carefully, as they are the backbone of the space – as well as being functional they should be clean-lined and space-enhancing. Large stone paving slabs, for example, are less fussy than small bricks, while a blonde-wood deck will reflect light better than a dark timber.

Follow the same space-making rules as those used inside, such as minimizing clutter, using pale colours and reflective materials, choosing cleverly designed furniture, and making the most of natural light (by positioning the seating area where it gets most sun, for example). You should also plan adequate storage, as you'll need somewhere to put barbecue and gardening equipment, at least, and possibly items such as deckchairs, loungers, half-used paint cans, household tools, and other DIY kit. A sentry-box-style shed will fit into even a tiny space, although there's nothing to stop you designing your own storage and having it built to fit.

Lighting for outside spaces Complete darkness outside your windows adds nothing to your home, whereas a beautifully lit, attractive outside area adds a view from the inside and immediately gives the impression of extra space. Installing lighting also allows you to use your outside space for longer, reveals otherwise unseen, shadowy corners, and draws the eye to the boundaries so that the floor area is extended as far as possible.

Left
This blonde-wood decked area, with its low-level, subtle planting and white furniture, is small yet manages to appear relatively spacious.

Opposite
Pierced metal steps and slender, mesh chairs make minimal impact here. Despite its rectangular outline and minimal planting, the garden still has a pleasantly organic feel thanks to the use of stone paving cut to an amoeba-like shape.

This is a brilliant example of clever planning. Glazed walls and doors link the inside to the outside, so that it all becomes one big living area. Plain stone slabs and low, slender, slatted-wood furniture ensure that the space looks as large as possible.

Opposite
Even with limited planting a tiny outside area can still be attractive and interesting. Here, a combination of pale wood, water, gravel, and metal have been used to convey a calm, Oriental atmosphere.

Good garden lighting follows the same basic rules as indoor lighting – it should provide general illumination of the space, light specific working areas such as patios and steps, highlight attractive features, and add drama by contrasting light and shade. In order to do this, you need to vary the sources and types of light, mixing larger and smaller spots, set at different levels, with wall lights and perhaps floor lights. You may want to include uplighters on spikes pushed into the ground, floodlights of different sizes, and wall washers, together with strings of fairy lights, solar-powered globes, and candles for interest.

Installing mains-powered exterior lighting is best done either during installation or an overhaul of the space, or at the time of year when the planting has died down the most – as the cables have to be buried very deep. There are stringent safety regulations that must be met so if you are in any doubt then ask a qualified electrician to do it.

Reflective and transparent materials To open up a small outside space, use as many see-through and reflective materials as possible. Balustrades and staircases could be made of glass, for example, as could sections of floor on roof terraces and balconies. Pierced metal and curvy wrought iron can also be useful for partially see-through screens and other boundaries. Mount large mirrors in strategic positions on fences and walls, with plants trailing around the edges, so that your space appears to double in size. You can also use mirror in unusual and eye-catching ways, such as at the back of niches in walls or in the form of a mosaic around the base of a water feature, so that it twinkles in the sun and reflects light prettily.

Choosing furniture It's not a good idea to cram a small outside area too full of furniture; on the other hand, you'll need somewhere to sit and

relax in comfort with friends. One easy option
is simply to bring out suitable furniture from
indoors, saving you both space and money.
Alternatively, buy outdoor furniture that either
folds or stacks when not in use, and remember
that if you don't have somewhere dry to store
it during winter it must be made of a durable,
weatherproof material.

Look for pieces that are minimal in style,
whether slatted wood, wire mesh, or moulded
plastic, on slender legs and without too much
decorative detailing. The aim is to minimize their
impact, so they could even be made from a
transparent material or be pierced with holes.
Furniture with a low, horizontal emphasis will
clear the space at eye level and so make it seem
larger; you could even just sit on floor cushions,
or simply throw down a picnic blanket. Finally, if
you have room for one you may want to consider
investing in a gas heater, which will give you
extended use of the space even in cooler weather.

Planting ideas It goes without saying that you
should not over-plant a small outside area if you
want it to look as big as possible. Plant clutter
is just as visually intrusive (if not more so) as
any other kind, so stick to species that are
proportionate to the space and, while varying
their heights for interest, avoid too many tall
plants that will give a jungle-like, claustrophobic
effect. Keep on top of the pruning, too. Depending
on how green-fingered you are, you may prefer
to limit planting in favour of a very architectural
space, or at least intersperse the plants with
paving, pebbles, or gravel.

Plants in pots are often a good idea in a
small garden, as they can be moved around as
necessary, though they do require meticulous
watering and regular re-potting if they are to
look their best. Avoid a mismatched collection of
pots, though, and instead choose a co-ordinating
selection of sleek, modern examples, perhaps
in galvanized steel, white ceramic, or zinc.
Slim beds may be a better choice for a keener
gardener, and can be dug with curvy outlines if
that suits the shape of your garden better. If you
really love gardening then don't restrict yourself to
ground level – use the walls as much as possible
with climbers on trellis or thin wire, hanging pots,
and rows of plants on tiered stands.

Real homes

A derelict meeting hall

Today it may be calm, quirky, and appealing, but when architect Ian Chee, of VX Design & Architecture, bought this property it was rather a mess. A former meeting hall that had been left derelict for years, it needed total re-organization inside: a mezzanine entrance level, a semi-basement that had been used for offices and storage, and an upper-floor meeting room with a raised stage area made poor use of what was a relatively large space, and failed to take advantage of the wonderful windows.

A radical re-design has converted the area into two spaces: a private lower floor with three bedrooms, two bathrooms, and a study, and a more public upper floor consisting of just one room – an open-plan kitchen, dining area, and space for relaxation. Chee has concealed a new staircase behind half-height walls, so that the space seems to go and on, while the

heating for the upper floor – in the form of a small but efficient radiator – is hidden below a wooden bench.

Architectural interventions aside, Chee's design offers many clever and less costly examples of how to make the most of both space and light in any home. The kitchen, for instance, can be separated from the rest of the upper floor using the simple device of large sheets of acrylic (almost, but not quite, see-through) on slider tracks. Storage is simple and straightforward: the kitchen cupboards form an L-shape, with both high and low units, and all appliances are neatly integrated. In the bedroom, cupboards have been built flush with the walls so that they are almost invisible, while in the sitting room a rank of "floating" shelves, painted the same colour as the walls, holds neat rows of CDs.

Left
A simple but brilliant idea, the glass-sided shower/bath is a *tour de force*; it transforms a tiny space into a highly functional yet beautiful bathroom.

Opposite
The bedroom has concealed cupboards built into the walls, and a wooden shutter at the high window. The bed, which Chee designed himself, features an integrated headboard and side tables.

The living area is flooded with light from the row of huge windows. White is the dominant colour, but bolder shades have been used to add character, combined with interesting patterns in the form of woven silk cushions, a zebra skin, and a soft rug.

Pale colours and contrasting textures provide the backbone of the house. A sliding panel made of frosted acrylic can be used to close off the kitchen from the open-plan living/dining area when necessary.

The furniture is a mix of old and new pieces, some made from recycled wood, others Chee's own design. For space-enhancing purposes most items are either minimal (such as the white sofa on slim legs), transparent (the glass coffee table), dual-purpose (the bed with integrated side tables), or can be tucked out of the way when not in use (the dining stools that slide under the table).

Everything in the house is unified by a colour scheme of white and natural shades (in particular dark wood), offset by the occasional dash of vivid colour. But even more than colour it is the textural choices that stand out, making a mostly monochromatic palette feel sensuous and warm. Texture provides the heart and soul of the house, from the wooden floor topped by soft rugs, and the smooth cupboard fronts that contrast with the patinated kitchen worktop, to the sleek glass that is offset by the tiny mosaic tiling in the bathroom.

In the downstairs rooms the windows are set high on the walls and Chee has fitted wooden shutters that fold right back when not needed. Upstairs he has used the simplest possible solution: white roller blinds that are so subtle as to be barely noticeable. During the daytime light pours in through these windows unimpeded; at night simple light-fittings are utilized, such as the tubes suspended from the upper kitchen cabinets, the pendant lamp at the opposite end of the sitting room, and the flexible lamp beside the bed.

However, Chee's cleverest creation by far is the glass-sided shower/bath – a gorgeous piece of design that combines both practicality and style. As an ingenious answer to the perennial question of how to fit both a shower and a bath into a tiny space, and make the result look good, it has all the hallmarks of a future design classic.

INSPIRATIONAL IDEAS

- White paint makes a great backdrop but can be cold and sterile if used exclusively. Adding touches of bolder colour, as illustrated here, does not detract from the sense of space but introduces warmth and interest.

- Texture is an important ingredient, providing a tactile sensuality to any space. Chee uses beautifully contrasting textures in every room, including wood, lacquer, glass, silk, and wicker.

- Window treatments are such that natural light is maximized throughout: the large windows in the living area have simple white roller blinds, while the bedroom's high windows can be concealed by wooden shutters.

- Clutter is carefully hidden away in specially designed storage – built-in cupboards in the bedroom, an L-shaped kitchen with both base and high units, and a rank of cantilevered shelves in the dining area.

- The fireplace is an ultra-simple hole-in-the-wall model that, while providing a focal point, does not intrude upon the surrounding space.

- Transparent and translucent surfaces are used in sensitive and imaginative ways, including the frosted acrylic sliding panel that can be used to close off the kitchen, the glass-sided shower/bath, and the glass coffee table.

- Each piece of furniture sits on slender legs, raising it off the ground and thus increasing the overall sense of space. The large and comfortable sofa is plain, pale, and minimal in style, blending into the background, while the slatted dining stools can simply be pushed under the delicate table when not in use. A long bench, made from recycled railway sleepers, is an effective way of concealing the radiator.

- The glass-sided shower/bath is a fabulous innovation; a wide ledge built at one side can be used for storing bathtime toiletries.

- The lighting throughout the house is extremely low-key. In the kitchen slim downlighters are suspended from the upper cupboards, providing good illumination for the worksurface, and in the bedroom a flexi-light can be positioned anywhere to provide comfortable reading in bed.

A dark basement flat

Few people would have the nerve to attempt the seemingly impossible task of turning a damp, dark, and dated basement into a comfortable, good-looking, modern family home. However, for architect Ian Hogarth it was an opportunity rather than a problem, a challenge to be relished – and one that he overcame with impressive flair.

His starting point was a basement flat that had been unchanged since the 1920s, with a concrete floor and walls that were dripping and peeling with damp. An extractor fan had to be on permanently just to alleviate the smell of mould. The plan was to turn it into a three-bedroom, two-bathroom property with a spacious living/dining/working area and a small courtyard. Every single modification, therefore, had to be carried out with the aim of maximizing space and increasing light levels.

The most radical part of the scheme was to knock down an entire interior wall in order to enlarge the living space and let in more light. (A warning: don't try this at home without advice from a structural engineer – Hogarth's wall supported four upper stories, and had to be replaced with a gargantuan metal beam.) The kitchen was then moved into the newly created corridor in order to free up space for an extra bedroom, and part of the rear roof was removed to create a courtyard that acts as a lightwell for the bedrooms.

The rest of the changes were less structural and more subtle, using every cunning trick in the book to make the home seem larger, lighter, and brighter. To save much-needed space Hogarth has avoided bulky radiators, instead fitting underfloor heating throughout. The whole house is painted gleaming white, and a poured-rubber floor installed everywhere except the master bedroom, which is laid with white shagpile carpet for retro-style comfort. In the open-plan living room a shelf-cum-bench-cum-fireplace has been specially designed to run the length of one wall, with cupboards underneath, while above the inset fireplace hangs a slender plasma-screen television, which can be hidden by the sliding doors of the capacious wall cupboards on each side. The cupboards are, naturally, all in

Left
By removing an inner wall Hogarth was able to move the kitchen into the corridor, freeing up space for an extra bedroom. On one side is the breakfast bar, on the other the working area. The corridor at the far end of the kitchen, which leads to the children's bedrooms, is brightened by colour-changing lighting.

Opposite
The living room can also be used for dining, parties, and work presentations. White floors and walls reflect the light, aided by the white-topped table next to the window. The fireplace-shelf has cupboards beneath, and the flat-screen TV above can be hidden by sliding doors.

white, though the shelf is made from grey-green slate – a salvage yard find and therefore not too expensive. The dining table, also a custom design, has a glossy white surface and is placed beside the window in order to bounce light around the rest of the room. It is surrounded by four white plastic Panton chairs, which not only look beautiful but provide a back-up for the table as light magnifiers. Around two sides of the room runs a huge, tomato-red, modular sofa that stands on slim metal legs – its jolt of colour is a welcome addition to the

otherwise all-white environment, making this a comfortable room in which to relax. The space is also useful for work presentations thanks to the large television and plentiful seating, and, what's more, can become a fabulous party venue simply by pushing the furniture to the edges of the room.

To fit an entire kitchen, complete with breakfast bar, into what is no more than a large corridor requires a certain amount of guile and ingenuity. To cut back on costs Hogarth has used glossy white Ikea cabinetry, but removed the base plinth so the

In the ensuite shower room a pair of shower heads saves time getting ready in the mornings. Wall-mounted fixtures cut down on clutter, while a sheet of mirror behind the basin reflects light.

units seem to float. All the appliances are neatly integrated and there is a white Corian worktop that incorporates a sink – its all-in-one look carefully planned so as to avoid visual interruptions that would detract from the space-making effect. On one side is the working area, with hob, cooker, and sink, while on the other is the breakfast bar: a recess fitted with the same glossy worksurface and mirrored at the back to reflect the light. Around the bar are floor-to-ceiling cupboards that provide masses of storage for all the kitchen equipment.

The corridor that leads from the kitchen to the children's bedrooms is the only area that receives no natural light at all, so Hogarth has installed a series of lights that change colour in sequence, washing the walls and floor with a rainbow-like effect. He continues the playful theme in the children's bathroom, which features an acrylic bath panel lit from behind by a pink striplight. The master ensuite shower room, covered

en masse in red mosaic tiles (bought from bankrupt stock so cheap to use), is more functional. It has two shower heads so that Ian and his partner, Claire, can save time getting ready in the mornings, a sheet of mirror behind the basin, and wall-mounted fittings that maximize the space.

In the master bedroom Hogarth has opted for highly charged decoration that ignores the room's small dimensions and lack of daylight in favour of dramatic colours and patterns, in order to create an intimate, bordello-like atmosphere. Nevertheless, he has carefully balanced the bold, colour-by-numbers painting and the purple chiffon curtains with white walls and carpet, an unfussy bed, spacious cupboards built around the bedhead, and wall-mounted, flexi-arm reading lights. On one wall Ikea wardrobes with mirror fronts appear to double the space – an illusion that, like the rest of the apartment, is bold, attractive, and stunningly effective.

Left
The master bedroom, quite deliberately, has less of an airy atmosphere than elsewhere in the house. However, despite its dark colours and bold patterns it does not feel claustrophobic, thanks to plentiful storage (including a wall of wardrobes with mirrored fronts) and white walls, carpet, and bedlinen.

INSPIRATIONAL IDEAS

- Moving the kitchen into the corridor was a masterpiece of lateral thinking, creating space for an extra bedroom. The kitchen itself, with floor-to-ceiling glossy white cupboards, a seamless white worktop, and integrated appliances, has plenty of room for storage and food preparation, while a small breakfast bar provides a place for informal meals.
- In the one area that has no natural daylight Hogarth has installed colour-change lighting to wash the walls and floor with rainbow-like patterns.
- The children's bathroom is small but perfectly formed. The sliding, space-saving door is made from frosted glass, offering privacy but light. A mirror runs along one entire wall, with a ladder radiator that holds towels; a wall-hung sink frees up floor space, and the bath has an extra-wide surround on which to place bathing essentials.

- The tiny inner courtyard garden has a fountain that can be illuminated at night. The children's bathroom looks directly onto it, and because no one can see in Hogarth has left the window bare.
- The living room contains a massive amount of storage but, because it is well-hidden below the shelf/fireplace and on the walls either side of the TV, it does not detract from the size or sleek appearance of the room.
- Televisions can be dreadful space guzzlers; however, a plasma screen hung on the wall takes up no space, and can easily be hidden by sliding doors when not in use.
- In the master bedroom Hogarth has fitted floor-to-ceiling mirrored wardrobes from Ikea to double the feeling of space, and used adhesive film to cover them in order to give the impression of sandblasted glass.

A newly-built city duplex

The most outstanding feature of this Spanish duplex apartment in Mataró is its perfect precision. From the monochromatic colour scheme to the clean-lined furniture, it is all cool, logical, and functional, pared-down to the absolute basics.

With clutter and fussy detailing banished, the way is clear for relaxed living. And while the apartment has been stripped of non-essentials, what is left is both good-looking and sensuously tactile. There may be no printed patterns or bold colours, but what remains are the enticing surfaces of brushed stainless steel, wood, porcelain, and glass, in natural tones and subtle textures, combined with soft white paint on all the walls and ceilings for maximum brightness. This is home comfort achieved with a view to calm, contemporary style.

Built on the site of a former factory, the apartment is one of a block of 26 designed by Toni Bou and Miquel Josep. However, during the build owner and architect Jaume Valor

modified the design to make the most of the space and light. On the lower floor is the living room/kitchen and bathroom, while upstairs is the bedroom (which leads directly onto a small terrace), a work studio, and another bathroom. In the block's basement Valor also has a small storage area, thus freeing up a huge amount of space in his apartment.

Valor's main move was to integrate the kitchen and living space into one large, open-plan room, with an enormous window running the entire length of one wall, which frames a view of nearby rooftops. With a large skylight above as well, this space is wonderfully bright and airy, and Valor has emphasized its luminosity by using pale colours and reflective surfaces in the form of stainless steel kitchen cupboards and a beech parquet floor. Raised high on tubular legs, the kitchen units echo the shapes of the modular sofa and matching footstool opposite, so that, instead of the usual bulky appearance, they

Opposite
For maximum luminosity, and to increase the flow between the spaces, the apartment is decorated completely in off-white, with natural wood and stainless steel throughout. The cherry-wood box is part-wardrobe, part-kitchen unit, and extra storage is built-in under the stairs.

Above
Valor has integrated the kitchen/dining/living room by eliminating walls, fitting the same flooring throughout, and choosing furniture that has a unity of design. The emphasis is on low, horizontal lines, even in the light bar that is suspended over the kitchen worksurface.

integrate seamlessly into the space. The emphasis is on low, lean, horizontal lines and smooth, shiny surfaces – nothing to interrupt the flow of light-filled space.

The living area is separated from the staircase by a dual-purpose unit made from elegant cherry wood: on one side it houses the cooker and further storage cupboards; on the other it is a large wardrobe. Mounted on a metal plinth, and not reaching quite up to the ceiling, it seems to float inconspicuously. More storage cupboards have been built-in under the open staircase, and a shallow bookcase, suspended

Right
The studio can be made more private by lowering the white motorized blind. Instead of a balustrade, Valor has used a column radiator.

on the wall at the base of the stairs, holds hundreds of books without intruding into any useful space.

The top floor can be open, or divided, as necessary, through the use of glass walls and motorized blinds that lower from the ceiling at the flick of a switch. The studio can convert into a second bedroom, or a portion of the bedroom can become a private dressing room. Continuing the theme of see-through surfaces, Valor has used a thick sheet of glass on one side of the stairwell, instead of a solid banister, and a radiator on the other side – an inspired solution.

The bed is typically modest – just a low divan with a plain cover – and is set against a wall covered in whitewashed pine boards. Either side of the bed are flexible reading lights and wall-hung baskets to hold bedside bits and pieces. To store clothes Valor has designed a wardrobe/dressing room concealed by a white pull-down blind. Covering an entire wall, it consists of a hanging rail with high shelves above that are neatly stacked with clear plastic boxes. Below are a couple of low, free-standing chests of drawers on tubular metal legs

that are reminiscent of the furniture downstairs. Another wall is in the form of a sliding glass door that leads onto a small terrace. Paved in pale stone, and planted with ordered rows of bamboo and bougainvillea in pots, it is a wonderful suntrap.

Adjoining the bedroom is the tiny bathroom, which would have no natural light were it not for the glass wall at one end that overlooks the staircase and studio. To increase the sense of space and light Valor has installed a pale vinyl floor, a massive sheet of mirror, and wall-mounted sanitaryware – complemented by sophisticated chrome and white fittings.

The remainder of the upper floor is taken up by Valor's studio, where a wall of delicate, custom-built shelving holds books, files, boxes, and a CD player. The office area is straightforward – a plain wooden desk, an elegant but practical swivel chair, and an adjustable lamp. However, for added comfort, and to really appreciate the views from his large window, Valor has placed a white canvas deckchair in one corner: the perfect spot in which to sit and plan further inspired, good-looking projects.

INSPIRATIONAL IDEAS

- Omitting interior walls and using the same style of flooring throughout makes a relatively small space much more fluid and connected. Here, Valor has chosen off-white paintwork and polished wood floors for maximum light reflectivity and a feeling of open airiness.

- This truly flexible space can be configured in different ways by simply raising or lowering motorized blinds. Valor has also used glass sheet, a column radiator, and a cherry wood storage unit as space dividers.

- When using a subdued colour palette it is important to concentrate on creating a pleasing variation of textures, such as the brushed metal, glass, and wood used here.

- Valor is lucky to have enormous windows, and he has made the most of them by ignoring conventional window treatments. Instead, louvred blinds on the outside can be lowered when necessary, for security and to block out the harsh sunshine.

- Almost all of Valor's furniture – including the kitchen cupboards – stands on thin legs or is wall-mounted. By increasing the visible floor space he has made each room appear as large as possible.

- A dual-purpose, custom-built cupboard positioned as a space-divider at the foot of the stairs can be accessed from both sides – one side as a wardrobe, the other as a kitchen unit that also contains a cooker.

- Valor's lighting is very subtle – small halogen spotlights built into the ceiling supplemented by a few fittings, which include a slender bar hung over the kitchen worktop, an adjustable desk lamp, and a pair of flexible reading lights either side of the bed.

- In order not to waste an inch of space, Valor has fitted custom-made storage under the stairs – the sizes of the cupboards varying to suit his requirements.

Left
The bedroom is small, but by mounting lights and bedside storage on the wall not an inch of space has been wasted. A glass wall allows natural light into the next-door bathroom.

A neglected 19th-century townhouse

When decorating a period home it can be tempting to become a slave to tradition – restoring or replicating original features without considering how they will fit into a 21st-century lifestyle. Many older homes already have plenty of nicely proportioned rooms, and even a garden, but they can sometimes be rather dark and claustrophobic. The key is to create a blend of old and new, retaining the best original features but not being afraid to introduce space-enhancing modern elements, too.

This Victorian townhouse in south-east London had been untouched for years and was full of character. However, the one thing it didn't have was a bright, airy atmosphere, and its owners were keen to alter the property in order to have a home that was at once elegant, up-to-date, and child-friendly. They commissioned architect Michael Phillips to help them make the necessary changes, and the result is a dramatic improvement from a cramped, dim, neglected old house to a delightful, open, and light-filled family home.

Phillips' first move was to open up the dark and cellular layout of the lower ground floor, moving the basement stairs and inserting a full-height sash window with shutters, to flood natural daylight down the new stairwell. He then designed a new, open-plan kitchen/dining/playroom area to connect through to the garden. He plotted the room around an island worktop/breakfast bar, fitting sleek white cupboards, both high and low,

Opposite
The glossy white kitchen units are sleek and modern, but their effect is softened by the use of warm wood for the worktops and floor. The room is lit by ceiling downlighters, supplemented by a row of pendants over the island unit.

Above
At the far end of the kitchen is the dining area, leading straight out onto the garden decking. With the sliding/folding glass doors, the entire space becomes one huge indoor-outdoor room.

for maximum storage capacity. One wall, the entire length of the lower ground floor, is devoted to ceiling-high cupboards, drawers, display shelving, and sliding panels for flexible storage. These match the ultra-modern kitchen cupboards, with their high-gloss finish and slim bar handles. The overall look is softened by the warmth of a golden wood floor and matching worksurface. At the front end of the house is a child's playzone, incorporating display shelving for "aesthetic" toys and concealed shelving for the rest. At the other end of the room is a dining area, with a simple wooden table, slat-back chairs, and a pair of benches. This leads directly onto the garden via a set of folding/sliding wood and glass doors. Immediately outside is a decked area, and when the doors are open this entire space becomes one enormous indoor-outdoor room. When the doors are closed a single curtain can be drawn to make the kitchen cosy, but most of the time it is pulled back well out of the way to allow

Above
The bathroom has a
luxurious feel despite
not being overly large.
Pale stone, off-white
walls, mirrors, and
a wall-hung basin
all contribute to
the impression of
generous space.

Opposite
The living room blends
old and new with panache.
The white walls and floors
give the room a clean
and airy feel, and form
a simple backdrop
to the detailed wood-
panelling of the window
shutters, the softly classic
furniture, and the sleek
flat-screen television.

daylight to pour in. At night illumination comes from downlighters in the ceiling and clean-lined pendants over the island unit.

In the kitchen the colour scheme is white and polished wood, with just a splash of brightness in the form of a large canvas painted by the owners' young daughter. The minimal, light-enhancing palette is continued throughout the entire house: white and pastel paints have been used liberally on walls, wood-work, mantelpieces, lamp bases, the floorboards of the sitting room, and even the rabbit hutch in the garden. The look is light and modern, but not overly so – the owners have chosen an eclectic mix of furnishings, including antiques and ethnic pieces, and included touches of soft colour here and there, so that the effect is easy on the eye and harmonious to live with.

The sitting room is almost entirely white or neutral, apart from a pretty lilac-upholstered sofa with pink cushions, and the bright covers of the books on the carved-wood coffee table (originally an Indian day bed). As always when designing a room in which space is emphasized, there is a balance between hiding all the clutter and creating an individual environment by displaying personal possessions. Here, some things have been left neatly on show, while others can be tidied into the specially built, white-painted cupboards that line one wall. And in a recess between the cupboards is a flat-screen television, which can be hidden by sliding a white-painted canvas panel across – a great example of how classic and contemporary go hand in hand.

Contrasting with such sleek technology, the room still has its original detailed cornices and wooden window shutters – the latter tuck right back into the window recesses to allow maximum daylight into the room. The furniture, both antique pieces and modern classic designs, complements the Victorian architecture but is far from being stuffy and formal. With pale upholstery, slender forms, and delicate legs, this is period style with a light touch, so it appears fresh and appealing as well as making the most of the space.

Upstairs the use of pale colours continues. The master bedroom is full of diffused light from the large windows covered with white voile panels, while a textured carpet and simple white bedlinen help to reflect the light. The tones of wood are pale (in the form of a new wooden bed) and distressed (an antique Swedish sofa with an elegantly carved timber frame and white upholstery), to set a mood of calm relaxation. In the main bathroom off-white walls are combined with walls of buff-coloured stone. A cantilevered stone slab forms the base for the shallow ceramic washbasin, with its sleek, wall-mounted tap; next to it is a small storage niche built into the outer wall of the house. The bath has been built with an extra-wide surround for displaying toiletries, and flanks a walk-in, doorless shower area. At the windows is a series of wooden Colonial-style shutters with louvres, which can be opened for light or angled for privacy. The end result is functional, attractive, and timelessly chic.

INSPIRATIONAL IDEAS

- The new sliding/folding glass doors that have replaced an exterior wall are the biggest innovation in this home. They transform the kitchen/diner, creating a huge indoor-outdoor space that's full of light and functions brilliantly for the family.
- The kitchen is spacious enough to be plotted around an island unit, which incorporates both storage and a worktop. High-gloss, white lacquer cupboards with stainless steel bar handles, and integrated appliances, make the room seem even bigger. The glossy surfaces reflect light around the room, but the overall feel is softened by the use of golden wood for the floor and worktops.
- There is masses of storage in the kitchen, with units fitted both high and low around the working area, and floor-to-ceiling cupboards, drawers, and shelves along an entire wall of the lower ground floor – plenty of room to hide kitchen equipment, crockery, cutlery, glassware, and children's toys.
- White and pale paints have been used for most surfaces around the house to present a clean-lined, fresh, and modern feel throughout.

- A wall of cupboards in the living room conceals clutter. To avoid having the television in a corner, which just wastes space, a recess has been created in which to hang a flat-screen TV that does not intrude into the room. It can even be covered when not in use by a sliding canvas panel.
- Instead of curtains the windows have shutters; during the daytime they fold neatly back out of the way.
- The living room furniture is a mix of old and new, but even the old does not look fussy and traditional. Everything is raised on legs, so the floor area seems larger, and the upholstery is in pale, contemporary colours.
- The bathroom consists of a sleek panelling of buff-coloured stone, off-white walls, a generously sized mirror, and chrome fittings. The limited colour palette gives the room a sophisticated look, emphasizing the feeling of space.
- The bathroom floor area is maximized by mounting a shallow bowl-shaped basin onto a stone slab cantilevered from the wall. A small storage niche tucks toiletries out of the way so they don't intrude upon the visual clarity of the room.

A cramped period apartment

That this desirable home looks very much like a cool, New York, loft-style apartment is somewhat deceptive – it is, in fact, situated on three floors of an Edwardian family house in north London. What's more, before its transformation into this streamlined space it was a warren of narrow corridors and tiny rooms – cramped, poky, and almost unpenetrated by natural light. However, the skill of architect and former owner David Mikhail has turned it into a light-filled, open, and desirable space, achieving penthouse style without bursting the bank balance.

The key was in knowing where to spend money and where to save it. Rationalizing the two bedrooms on the top floor into one large bedroom with an ensuite bathroom, and then adding a small, glass-enclosed balcony, was costly but worth every penny in terms of gaining the luxury of some outside space. Re-plastering all the walls to a smooth-as-silk finish was also pricey (and time-consuming), and laying a new ash floor

throughout was another expensive element. However, these latter two features have provided the structure and backbone of the property: they make the spaces flow uninterruptedly, and reflect light around the apartment to superb effect. To increase light levels and the feeling of openness even further, Mikhail enlarged the doorways and replaced the wall between the living room and kitchen/diner with a massive sliding door.

At the opposite end of the scale were a variety of modest and straightforward, yet nevertheless highly effective, measures. Mikhail decided to paint all the walls and ceilings in the most economical paint of all: white emulsion. This allowed him to pick out small areas in bolder colours, including gorgeous polished-plaster wall treatments by an artist friend, without detracting from the overall feeling of airy brightness. He fitted standard halogen downlighters in all the ceilings, plus a few plug-in lamps that can be turned on and off individually. He

The open-plan kitchen-dining area contains a glass-topped table and Eames chairs that can be stacked up when not in use. The cupboards have a simple Ikea framework with MDF doors. Lights concealed below the wall cupboards illuminate the stainless-steel worktop.

The harmonious mix of whites and natural tones, with textures from smooth to soft and shaggy, makes this living room feel ultra-comfortable. The lean, low furniture is minimal in impact, and clutter is stored in a pair of slim, floor-to-ceiling cupboards at one end of the room.

installed plain white sanitaryware in the bathroom, complemented by luxurious circular mosaic tiles and stylish, wall-mounted taps. The hole-in-the-wall fireplaces look incredibly upmarket but actually were made rather cheaply from concrete and lime render, finished with a simple grate. And for the kitchen cupboards Mikhail used Ikea carcasses, fronted by doors made from sheets of medium-density fibreboard and finished with long, slim, metal handles. These base and wall units run the length of the room, incorporating a built-in sink and cooker, and provide masses of storage with the minimum of impact.

Storage in the sitting room (for books, videos, and so on) is not in the place one might expect – in the alcoves on either side of the chimney breast – but is, instead, concealed in the walls that flank the sliding door. This ingenious solution takes up practically no space while hiding masses of clutter. In the attic bedroom all the mess can go behind a curtain on a track at the edge of the room, while in the bathroom anything unsightly can be put away in slender, built-in, MDF cupboards that are painted the same colour as the walls.

This careful planning leaves each room feeling calm and uncluttered, and the uninterrupted spaces are further emphasized by the furniture, which is a mix of one or two designer classics, some junk shop finds, and a range of high-street bargains. It is universally pale in colour and plain in style, with a concentration on low, horizontal lines that make the most of the high ceilings. From the modular sofa on delicate steel legs to the bentwood bedroom chair, the Eames dining chairs that stack conveniently out of the way to the low tables on castors, each piece is comfortable, functional, attractive, and space-enhancing. Mikhail also used transparent and reflective materials in clever ways, including a stainless steel worktop and splashback in the kitchen, a glass-topped dining table, acrylic splashbacks and plenty of mirror in the bathroom, and a metal laundry bin in the bedroom.

Mikhail was lucky to have attractive views, and thanks to the new floor-to-ceiling balcony doors he could see nothing but trees and sky from his bed, so he decided to leave all his windows completely bare. For modesty's sake he could wheel a folding screen across the bedroom window, but otherwise he didn't worry about the neighbours and just relished the light that pours in from dawn until dusk throughout this seamless, streamlined, easy-going home.

Opposite
Adding a balcony with large sliding doors to the top-floor bedroom was the most costly element in Mikhail's project, but was worth the expense and effort. The room is furnished with modest but attractive pieces that bring colour, texture, and character to the scheme.

Above
In the all-white ensuite bathroom Mikhail fitted inexpensive sanitaryware, complemented by circular mosaic tiles and acrylic splashbacks and surfaces. Storage is concealed carefully in slim, built-in wooden cupboards that line the walls.

INSPIRATIONAL IDEAS

- Using white emulsion throughout is not only economical, but is the best way to reflect light through the apartment. Mikhail softened it with touches of colour and a pleasing variety of textures, including a shaggy rug, a wicker basket, and velvet upholstery.
- Polished ash floorboards, used everywhere except the bedroom, really help to unify and streamline the entire space, as well as providing an expanse of reflective, glossy surface.
- A complete absence of curtains or blinds simplifies the rooms and allows light to flood in; a screen at the bedroom window provides privacy when necessary.
- A floor-to-ceiling sliding door connects the living room and kitchen, making it one big, open-plan space that is lit by windows at each end.
- The lack of clutter is down to well-thought-out storage in every room. Mikhail's most innovative idea was the floor-to-

ceiling cupboards in the recesses of the sliding doors between the living room and kitchen. The result is maximum capacity, but no wasted space.
- The kitchen-diner is compact but every inch has been made to count. Inexpensive but good-looking cupboards run along an entire wall, incorporating a built-in sink and cooker, and downlighters are set into the base of the upper units. The dining table is made of glass, and the chairs can be stacked up when not needed.
- To emphasize a sense of space the best furniture is pale in colour, slender in shape, and simple in design – comfortable yet unobtrusive. Here, each piece adheres to these rules, while retaining a subtle character.
- The bathroom makes use of inexpensive fittings combined with mosaic tiles on the walls and floor. In a small space it is possible to use expensive elements to add a touch of luxury.

A small attic

This attic apartment in Barcelona was once a jigsaw puzzle of small rooms, each of them darker and gloomier than the next – the whole arrangement simply emphasized how tiny the space was. When new owners took it over as a holiday home they wanted the property to feel less enclosed and more comfortable for modern living. They wanted it to be light and bright, and, in particular, to make the most of its gloriously sunny terrace.

The solution, though radical, was pretty straightforward: architects Ellen Rapelius and Xavier Franquesa simply ripped out almost all the internal partitions, turning the apartment into one large living/dining/cooking/sleeping room that leads directly onto the terrace, with a bijoux shower room and toilet tucked away to one side. That the new multi-functional space is open and connected, yet also cleverly separated so that each activity has its own demarcated area, is thanks to two devices. First, there are clear changes of floor level between the spaces, creating rooms within the room; second, there is a carefully controlled rhythm of colour, pattern, and surface texture that results in a harmonious flow from area to area, while still demonstrating the different purposes.

The living space is furnished with a low-slung, lightly upholstered sofa, a slender reading lamp, a floor cushion, and a series of shiny plastic storage boxes that are piled up to make a coffee table. Through a pair of floor-to-ceiling glass doors is the terrace, where the green, white, and terracotta colour theme continues. The clay tiles outside were the starting point for the colour of the vinyl flooring that runs through the entire flat – a bold choice, tempered by the use of white for the walls and most of the furnishings. Sheer voile curtains at the windows filter the sometimes harsh Mediterranean light, but otherwise these two spaces are simply one comfortable, light-filled living area.

To the other side the dining area and kitchen are set on a lower level, with the walls of the dining space covered in white, retro-style paper, and those of the kitchen protected by white-

glazed ceramic tiles. Standing on slender metal legs the dining table is also white, its glossy surface acting as an efficient light-reflector; the chairs are white with green, echoing the pistachio-and-orange colour theme that both unifies and separates each section. The apartment is lit by inset ceiling downlighters, but over the dining table there is an original 1970s pendant lamp, in plain white but with an intriguing, origami-like surface.

The kitchen concentrates on practicality rather than making a statement, and consists of a single galley of basic, white-fronted cupboards, with a sink, hob, and dishwasher built-in.

Opposite
By removing the interior walls the architects have created a living/cooking/eating/sleeping space that leads directly onto the sunny terrace and is full of Mediterranean light. The different functions of each area are delineated by a change in floor level and wall treatment.

Above
The kitchen is extremely simple, just a row of white base and wall units with integrated appliances, and a microwave hung on the wall to one side. The dining area is adjacent to the kitchen, on the same level but marked by retro-style geometric wallpaper.

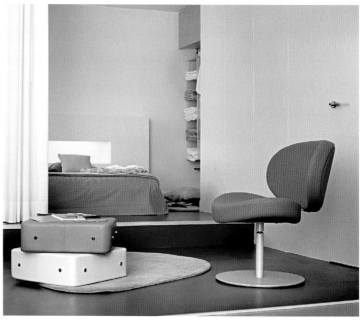

Above

The bathroom is
extremely compact,
but its careful, simple
design means that it
is entirely comfortable
and practical to use,
with plenty of space
to manoeuvre.

Above right

The bedroom is
separated from the
rest of the apartment
by a change of floor
level, and for privacy
a voile curtain can
be pulled across
when necessary.

A small microwave is fixed tidily, at eye level, on the wall to one side. The bedroom is right next door, but seems totally separate thanks to a step up that sets it on a higher level, and a half-height storage unit that partially blocks it off from the rest of the room. When necessary, a voile curtain (suspended from a simple ceiling track) can be drawn right across for intimacy.

Furniture throughout the property has been restricted to only what is really necessary, and each piece is straightforward in style – clean-lined and unfussy. The bedroom is no exception: the bed is a rectangular platform, with a plain orange cover that complements the colours elsewhere, and a large, built-out rectangle as a headboard that incorporates a backlit storage niche. Its low, horizontal lines echo those of the bed itself, while the lighting draws the eye into the space and emphasizes the length of the apartment as a whole. The wardrobe is a row of high cupboards with an open rail beneath and a shelf hung close to the floor. A canvas hanging rack can hold folded sweaters, underwear, linen, or spare towels, while anything too untidy can be hidden behind the cupboard doors above.

The bathroom is the only properly enclosed room in the apartment, and is a good example of how to squeeze the maximum use out of the smallest space. In little more than the floor area of a closet there is a toilet, basin, and shower. Pale colours, a wall-hung basin, sheet mirror with a light above, and a glass shower door help prevent a feeling of claustrophobia. Open storage space on the side of the basin fits neatly into one corner. The apartment has been designed to look effortlessly simple – an integrated, flowing whole that provides ordered spaces for living, and maximum daylight in every possible corner.

INSPIRATIONAL IDEAS

- The key idea in this apartment was to take down all interior divisions to allow light from the terrace to illuminate every corner. The shower room is the only area separated by walls.
- In a one-room home it is important to demarcate what activities take place in which areas. Here, the different floor levels divide the space while still connecting it, a clever device that is echoed by the variation in surface textures and the use of spots of bright colour that run from area to area.
- The rustic floor colour is taken from the clay tiles of the terrace, so that inside and outside are clearly linked. However, the effect is toned down by the use of bright white walls, ceilings, and furnishings.
- It is important not to cram a really tiny space with too much furniture. In this property there is the bare minimum for comfortable living, all of it slender in form and subtly designed, and without fussy detailing.
- When you have an outside area that is adjacent to a small interior it's a good idea to try to link them as much as possible. The floor-to-ceiling glass doors here not only allow plenty of light into all corners of the apartment, but also offer a view that really expands the space.
- Window treatments for a small room should be kept as simple as possible: the white voile curtains here blend well into the background.
- Lighting design may seem a complex art, but it can be very straightforward. Here, ceiling downlighters provide the main illumination, supplemented by a pendant light over the dining table and a floor-standing reading lamp beside the sofa.
- The bedroom storage is, unusually, in the form of a hanging rail with a shelf below. High up, there is a row of cupboards into which unsightly things can be tucked, but on the whole, most clothing will be on show. This is not generally advisable as it can look very messy, but it does at least mean that a great deal of extra floor space remains visible here, making the room appear larger.
- The headboard is a clever device, with a storage niche incorporated and a light that draws the eye to the far end of the apartment, therefore emphasizing its size.

Left
Double doors open onto the sunny terrace, where the terracotta, white, and green colour scheme echoes that of the whole apartment.

STORAGE

The Cotswold Company
Tel: 0870 241 0973 for mail order
www.cotswoldco.com

CubeStore
Charlwoods Road
East Grinstead
Surrey RH19 2HP   UK
Tel: 01342 310033 for mail order

Hold Everything
PO Box 7807
San Francisco
CA 94120   USA
Tel: 800 421 2285
www.holdeverything.com

The Holding Company
243–245 Kings Road
London SW3 5EL   UK
Tel: 020 7352 1600
www.theholdingcompany.co.uk

Inventory
26–34 Kensington High Street
London W8 4PF   UK
Tel: 020 7937 2626 for branches

ONE-STOP SHOPS

ABC Carpet & Home
Tel: 561 279 7777 for nearest US store
www.abchome.com

Aram
110 Drury Lane
London WC2B 5SG   UK
Tel: 020 7557 7557
www.aram.co.uk

Bhs
Tel: 020 7262 3288 for UK branches
www.bhs.co.uk

The Conran Shop
Michelin House
81 Fulham Road
London SW3 6RD   UK
Tel: 020 7589 7401
www.conran.com
and
407 East 59th Street
New York
NY 10022   USA
Tel: 212 755 9079
www.conran.com

Crate & Barrel
Tel: 800 927 9202 for nearest US store
www.crateandbarrel.com

Geoffrey Drayton
85 Hampstead Road
London NW1 2PL   UK
Tel: 020 7387 5840
and
104 High Street
Epping
Essex CM16 4AF   UK
Tel: 01992 573929
www.geoffrey-drayton.co.uk

Dwell
264 Balham High Road
London SW17 7AN   UK
Tel: 0870 241 8653
www.dwell.co.uk

Habitat
Tel: 0845 6010 740 for branches
www.habitat.net.

Heal's
196 Tottenham Court Road
London W19 9LD   UK
Tel: 020 7636 1666
www.heals.co.uk

Ikea UK
Tel: 020 8208 5600 for branches
www.ikea.co.uk

Ikea USA
Tel: 847 969 9700 or 800 434 4532
for nearest store
www.ikea-usa.com

InHouse
28 Howe Street
Edinburgh EH3 6TG   UK
Tel: 0131 225 2888
and
24-26 Wilson Street
Glasgow G1 1SS   UK
Tel: 0141 552 5902

John Lewis Partnership
Tel: 020 7629 7711 for UK branches
www.johnlewis.com

Laura Ashley
Tel: 0870 5622116 for UK branches;
or 0871 230 2301 for mail order
www.lauraashley.com

Lloyd Davies
81 King Street
Manchester M2 4ST   UK
Tel: 0161 832 3700
www.lloyddavies.co.uk

Momentum
31 Charles Street
Cardiff CF10 2GA   UK
Tel: 029 2023 6266
www.momentumcardiff.com

Muji
Tel: 020 7792 8283 for UK branches
www.muji.co.uk

Ocean
Freepost LON811
London SW18 4BR   UK
Tel: 01993 770564
www.oceanuk.com

OKA Direct Ltd
Chene Court
Poundwell Street
Modbury
Devon PL21 0QJ   UK
Tel: 0870 160 6002
www.okadirect.com

Pier One Imports
71 Fifth Avenue
New York
NY 10003   USA
Tel: 212 206 1911
www.pier1.com

Pottery Barn
Tel: 800 922 9934 for nearest US store
www.potterybarn.com

Purves & Purves
220–224 Tottenham Court Road
London W1T 7QE   UK
Tel: 020 7580 8223
www.purves.co.uk

Restoration Hardware
935 Broadway
New York
NY 10011   USA
Tel: 800 762 1005
www.restorationhardware.com

Selfridges
400 Oxford Street
London W1A 1AB   UK
Tel: 020 7629 1234
www.selfridges.co.uk

LIGHTING

Aktiva Systems
10 Spring Place
London NW5 3BH   UK
Tel: 020 7428 9325
www.aktiva.co.uk

Anglepoise
Tel: 01527 63771 for UK stockists
www.anglepoise.com

Artemide
106 Great Russell Street
London WC1B 3LJ   UK
Tel: 020 7631 5200
www.artemide.com

Babylon Design
301 Fulham Road
London SW10 9QH   UK
Tel: 020 7376 7233
www.babylonlondon.com

Best & Lloyd
Tel: 0121 558 1191 for UK stockists
www.bestandlloyd.co.uk

Chelsea Lighting Design
Unit 1
23a Smith Street
London SW3 4EJ   UK
Tel: 020 7824 8144

Christopher Wray
591-593 Kings Road
London SW6 2YW   UK
Tel: 020 7736 8434
www.christopherwray.com

John Cullen Lighting
585 Kings Road
London SW6 2EH   UK
Tel: 020 7371 5400
www.johncullenlighting.co.uk

London Lighting Co
135 Fulham Road
London SW3 2RT   UK
Tel: 020 7589 3612

Mr Resistor
82–84 New Kings Road
London SW6 4LU   UK
Tel: 020 8874 2234
www.mr-resistor.co.uk

FURNITURE

BoConcept® UK Ltd
158 Tottenham Court Road
London W1 7NH   UK
Tel: 020 7388 2447
www.boconcept.co.uk

Channels
1–3 New Kings Road
London SW6 4SB   UK
Tel: 020 7371 0301
www.channelsdesign.com

Charles Page Furniture
61 Fairfax Road
London NW6 4EE
Tel: 020 7328 9851
www.charlespage.co.uk

Highly Sprung
Tel: 020 7924 1124 for UK branches
www.highlysprung.co.uk

Hitch Mylius
Tel: 020 8443 2616 for UK stockists
www.hitchmylius.com

Ligne Roset
Tel: 0845 602 0267 for UK stockists
www.ligne-roset.co.uk

Loft
Simpsons Fold, 24–28 Dock Street
Leeds LS10 1JF   UK
Tel: 0113 305 1515

Noel Hennessy
6 Cavendish Square
London W1G 0PD   UK
Tel: 020 7323 3360
www.noelhennessy.com

Sharps Bedrooms
Tel: 0800 789789
For more information, or to book a free
design consultation, call 0800 917 8178
or visit www.sharps.co.uk

Sofa Workshop
Tel: 01443 238699 for UK branches
www.sofaworkshop.co.uk

Twentytwentyone
274 Upper Street
London N1 2UA   UK
Tel: 020 7288 1996
www.twentytwentyone.com

SPECIALISTS

Eclectics
Tel: 01843 608789
www.eclectics.co.uk
Made-to-measure blinds, panels,
and curtains

Hideaway Beds Ltd
Unit 1, Bell Close
Plympton
Plymouth PL7 4JH   UK
Tel: 01752 511111
www.hideaway.co.uk

KitchenBath.com
738 Franklin Avenue, Suite B
Franklin Square
NY 11010   USA
Tel: 800 646 1305
www.lasalesco.com

Pilkington
Tel: 01744 28882 for UK branches
www.pilkington.com
International glass and glazing
manufacturers

Spiral Staircase Systems
Tel: 01273 858341
www.spiralstairs.co.uk

Tiltaway
1390 N Rugby Road
Hendersonville, NC 28791   USA
Tel: 877 85458 233
www.tiltaway.com
Foldaway wall beds

Valcucine
Via L. Savio 11
33170 Pordenone   Italy
Tel: 0434 517 911
www.valcucine.it
Kitchens and kitchen accessories

Velux Company Ltd
Woodside Way
Glenrothes East
Fife KY7 4ND   UK
Tel: 0870 166 7676
www.velux.co.uk

Velux America Inc
PO Box 5001
Greenwood, SC 29648   USA
Tel: 800 88 83589
www.velux-america.com

Acknowledgments

Mitchell Beazley would like to acknowledge and thank the following for kindly supplying images for publication in this book:

Front cover Mainstream/Paul Massey, architect John Pawson
Back cover top right Red Cover/Adrian Wilson, **below left** Red Cover/Jake Fitzjones, **below right** Andreas Von Einsiedel/Elena & Glyn Emrys

2 Mainstream/Darren Chung; 4–5 Red Cover/Henry Wilson, architect Ian Chee; 6 Octopus Publishing Group/John Merrell; 8 Bo Concept; 10 Andreas von Einsiedel, architect Richard Rodgers, interior design Anna French; 11–12 Mainstream/Ray Main; 13 Red Cover/Tim Evan-Cook; 14 Mainstream/Ray Main; 15 Red Cover/Verity Welstead; 16 Octopus Publishing Group/ M. Banks; 17 View/Chris Gascoigne; 18 Mainstream/Ray Main; 19 Mainstream/Ray Main, architect Glyn Emrys; 20 Mainstream/ Ray Main, architect McDowell & Benedetti; 21 Red Cover/ James Mitchell; 22 Crown Paints (www.crownpaints.co.uk); 23 Arcaid.co.uk/Trevor Mein; 24 Mainstream/Ray Main, architect Wells Mackereth; 25 Red Cover/Homebase; 26 Arcaid.co.uk/ Richard Powers; 27 Red Cover/Winfried Heinze; 28 Red Cover/ Grey Crawford; 29 **left** Red Cover/Douglas Gibb, **right** Oka Direct; 30 Sharps Bedrooms; 31 Mainstream/Ray Main; 32 Sofa Workshop; 33 Andreas von Einsiedel, architect and interior design Hugh Jacobsen; 34 **above** Octopus Publishing Group/Dominic Blackmore, **below** Mainstream/Ray Main, courtesy London & Country Homes; 35 Octopus Publishing Group/Sebastian Hedgecoe; 36 Crown Paints (www.crownpaints.co.uk); 37 Red Cover/Adrian Wilson; 38 Andreas von Einsiedel, architect Piers Gough; 39 Red Cover/Henry Wilson; 40 Arcaid.co.uk/Richard Bryant, architect D'Soto Architects; 41 **above** Andreas von Einsiedel, architect and interior design Bernd Kuenne, **below** Laura Ashley; 42 Red Cover/Henry Wilson; 43 Spiral Staircase Systems; 44 Red Cover/Ken Hayden; 45 Red Cover/Winfried Heinze; 46 Eclectics; 47 Red Cover/Ed Reeve; 48 Eclectics; 49 Red Cover/Henry Wilson; 50 Andreas von Einsiedel, architect David Walker, interior design Ruth Aram; 51 Mainstream/Ray Main; 52 Red Cover/Winfried Heinze; 53 **above** Red Cover/Winfried Heinze, **below** Mainstream/Ray Main; 54 Eclectics; 55 Octopus Publishing Group/James Merrell; 56 Octopus Publishing Group/ Sebastian Hedgecoe; 57 Red Cover/Andrew Twort; 58–59 Mainstream/Ray Main; 60 Mainstream/Ray Main, architect Nico Rensch; 61 Laura Ashley; 62 Mainstream/Ray Main, courtesy Robin Guild; 63 Red Cover/Simon McBride; 64 Mainstream/Ray Main, architect Julie Richards@msn.com; 65 **left** Ocean, **right** Mainstream/Ray Main, architect Circus Architects; 66 John Lewis plc; 68–69 Mainstream/Ray Main, designer Joseph; 70 Red Cover/Verity Welstead; 71 Andreas von Einsiedel, architect Thomas Griem; 72 Red Cover/Ed Reeve; 73 Ikea; 74–75 Andreas von Einsiedel, architect: Reinhard Weiss; 76 Mainstream/Ray Main, courtesy Plain & Simple Kitchens; 77 Andreas von Einsiedel, interior design Konstantine & Toma von Haften, Coconut Company; 78 Red Cover/Jake Fitzjones; 79 View/Richard Glover, interior designer Ivan Bussens; 80 **above** Mainstream/Ray Main/courtesy Idyom-Milan, **below** Red Cover/Jake Fitzjones; 81 Valcucine; 82 Narratives/Jan Baldwin; 83 View/Richard Glover, architect Arthur Collin; 84–85 Red Cover/Jake Fitzjones; 86 Arcaid.co.uk/ Richard Bryant; 87 Red Cover/Winfried Heinze; 88 Red Cover/ Chris Tubbs; 89 Red Cover/Steve Dalton; 90 Hulsta (www.hulsta.nl); 91 Mainstream/Ray Main; 92–93 Andreas von Einsiedel, interior designer Michael Reeves; 94 Red Cover/Robin Matthews; 95–96 Red Cover/Ed Reeve; 97 Red Cover/Winfried Heinze; 98 Mainstream/Darren Chung, courtesy Ripples Bathrooms; 99 Red Cover/Verity Welstead; 100 Red Cover/Andrew Twort; 101 **above** Red Cover/Henry Wilson, **below** Andreas von Einsiedel, architect Thomas Griem; 102–103 Mainstream/Ray Main; 104 Red Cover/Tim Evan-Cook; 105 Red Cover/Henry Wilson; 106 Ocean; 107 Mainstream/Ray Main; 108–109 Ikea; 110 Red Cover/Adrian Wilson; 111 Red Cover/Henry Wilson; 112 Red Cover/Winfried Heinze; 113 Red Cover/Ken Hayden; 114 Michael Phillips; 116–119 Red Cover/Henry Wilson, architect Ian Chee; 120 Red Cover/Tom Scott, architect Hogarth Architects; 121 Interior Archive/Simon Upton, architect Hogarth Architects; 122 Red Cover/Chris Tubbs, architect Hogarth Architects; 123 Red Cover/Tom Scott, architect Hogarth Architects; 124–127 RBA Revistas SA/Eugeni Pons; 128–131 Michael Phillips, Baxter Phillips Architects; 132 David Mikhail Architects/Julian Cornish Trestrail; 133–134 David Mikhail Architects/Paul Massey, courtesy Living Etc; 135 David Mikhail Architects/Julian Cornish Trestrail; 136–137 Ellen Rapelius and Xavier Franquesa/Jordi Miralles; 138 **left** Ellen Rapelius and Xavier Franquesa, **right** Ellen Rapelius and Xavier Franquesa/Jordi Miralles; 139 Ellen Rapelius and Xavier Franquesa.

Please note that retailers credited above cannnot guarantee the availability of goods featured in this book.

Mitchell Beazley would like to thank the following people for additional editorial work on the book:
Proofreader – Claire Musters
Indexer – Helen Snaith

The architects featured in the Real homes section of the book are:
Ian Chee VX Design & Architecture – www.vxdesign.com
Hogarth Architects – Tel: 020 7565 8366; Email: info@hogartharchitects.co.uk; www.hogartharchitects.co.uk
David Mikhail Architects – Tel: 020 7377 8424; Email: info@davidmikhail.com; www.davidmikhail.com
Jaume Valor – Tel: 093 798 9001; Email: valor.arq@coac.es
Michael Phillips, partner at Baxter Phillips Architects – Tel: 020 7924 5837; www.bp-architects.co.uk
Ellen Rapelius and Xavier Franquesa – Email: info@stnex.com; www.stnex.com